mind
over
batter

mind

75 RECIPES for
BAKING as THERAPY

batter

over

JACK HAZAN, MA, LMHC

With Michael Harari

Photography by Lauren Volo

CHRONICLE BOOKS

SAN FRANCISCO

Library of Congress Cataloging-in-Publication Data available.

ISBN 978-1-7972-1230-2

Manufactured in China.

Design by Rachel Harrell.
Photography by Lauren Volo.
Typesetting by Frank Brayton.
Food styling by Marianna Velasquez.
Prop styling by Maeve Sheridan.

Alexa and Amazon Echo are registered trademarks of Amazon Technologies, Inc. Bob's Red Mill is a registered
trademark of Bob's Red Mill Natural Foods, Inc. CliffsNotes is a registered trademark of Course Hero, Inc. Cointreau
is a registered trademark of COINTREAU Société par actions simplifiée. Costco is a registered trademark of Costco
Wholesale Membership, Inc. Entenmann's is a registered trademark of Bimbo Bakeries USA, Inc. Grand Marnier is
a registered trademark of Marnier-Lapostolle Bisquit société anonyme. Häagen-Dazs is a registered trademark of
HDIP, Inc. Instagram is a registered trademark of Instagram, LLC. Junior Mints is a registered trademark of Tootsie
Roll Industries, LLC. Kahlua is a registered trademark of The Absolut Company. Marvel is a registered trademark of
Marvel Characters, Inc. Nilla Wafers is a registered trademark of Nabisco. Oreo is a registered trademark of Mondelez
International. Pepperidge Farms is a registered trademark of Pepperidge Farm, Incorporated. Pinterest is a registered
trademark of Pinterest, Inc. Ritalin is a registered trademark of Novartis AG. Splenda is a registered trademark of
Heartland Consumer Products, LLC. Twix is a registered trademark of Mars, Inc. Xanax is a registered trademark of
Pharmacia & Upjohn Company.

Disclaimer: This book is not intended to be a replacement for therapy.
If you are in need, please speak with a licensed professional.

10 9 8 7 6 5 4 3 2 1

Chronicle books and gifts are available at special quantity discounts to
corporations, professional associations, literacy programs, and other
organizations. For details and discount information, please contact our
premiums department at corporatesales@chroniclebooks.com or at
1-800-759-0190.

Chronicle Books LLC
680 Second Street
San Francisco, California 94107
www.chroniclebooks.com

This book is dedicated to the women in my life, who have been
my biggest fans and teachers throughout the years. You've
helped me realize my own power—in and out of the kitchen—
and have helped shape me into the man, baker, and therapist
I am today. I love you all.

To my mother, Sharon Hazan, for being
an inspiration in the kitchen.

In honor of Grandma Raquel Benun.

In loving memory of Grandma Peggy Hazan.

CONTENTS

Notes from a Baking Therapist 8

Self-Care 22

Mindfulness 56

Finding Comfort 96

Dealing with Stress and Anxiety 130

Letting Go of Frustration 166

Connecting with Others 200

Finding Joy 234

Acknowledgments 267

Index 269

Welcome to baking as therapy. I'm Jack—a licensed psychotherapist, MA, LMHC—and I'll be your guide on this healing journey through easy-to-make, deliciously decadent, sweet and savory treats!

You might be wondering, "What exactly is Baking Therapy, Jack?" or "What does this therapist know about baking?" Baking isn't just a chore, or something you should be doing for a celebration—it's much more layered than that. At its core, Baking Therapy is an innovative approach to some of the most commonly presented issues I see as a licensed therapist. It's a type of therapy that engages all of your senses, is available at your fingertips, and in your own home, even if you've never realized it before. Baking your way through tough feelings helps you break down what you're going through in a digestible way. (Heads up: Get ready for a few too many food puns.)

Before I became a therapist, my life laid out the ingredients to practice Baking Therapy. Imagine a table filled with mise en place, with each ingredient representing a different part of my story, waiting to be mixed together to make me who I am. The same (I hope) can be said for you and why you're here! Let's get started—and bake what your momma gave ya.

Be True to All of You

I come from a very traditional family—and community. Born and raised in the Syrian Jewish community in Brooklyn, New York, I always thought, "Where do I belong?" Forget about the black sheep. I was the gold-plated (marzipan) duck. I didn't care about sports. I had a colorful personality. I adore the community I was born into, and I know that they adore me as well. But growing up, finding my place wasn't easy. There were expectations—practically set in stone— from the minute I was born, if not before.

My grandparents were first-generation immigrants from Syria. They were kicked out of their country just for being Jewish. They came to an entirely new country, with a new foreign culture, with no money, no connections, and no idea what tomorrow would bring. That uncertainty must've been such a burden. But my grandfather, like many of his fellow countrymen, set out to work hard to provide for his family. When hardships hit him, he never gave up. Lo and behold, he worked his way to owning a building on Fifth Avenue. (Talk about creating the dream!)

He, like many fellow Syrian Jewish immigrant men, was driven by one thing: a desire to not fail. They couldn't afford to not succeed in this new world after being forced from their old one. The community came together with the intention of creating a home, not only for them, but also for their families and future generations. They created—in abundance—financial security, community centers, and interpersonal relationships. They established themselves as true

New Yorkers, becoming an affluent community in the process. This meant that they were wary of things that might challenge the community they had so painstakingly built up.

Enter me! (Insert nervous laughter.) I was expected to go to Jewish school (yeshiva) and grow up to have a wife and 4 kids (none of that nuclear family with *only* 2.5 kids). I was meant to go into the family business, eventually take over, and pass it down to my sons. That was all part of the "plan." Yet there I was—ADHD, hyperactive, and (too young to realize I was yet) gay—practically throwing the proverbial wrench into their conservative community. These traits and characteristics weren't talked about, so I didn't know who I could confide in and whom I could be my authentic self with. I wanted people to like me, so I put on my best face for the community.

My parents guided me to be able to experience the same sense of safety of community and prosperity. But what happens when you try to mix oil and water? Sure, if you blend them, it looks like they eventually come together. But appearances can be deceiving; they'll separate the first chance they get. For me, I knew I had to find my place—my community—and it might not be the one I was born into. That was a hard pill for my parents to swallow because the Syrian Jewish community was all they knew. It's what they wanted for me, no matter how different the community and I are.

Yeshiva felt like a stricter version of the community: If you didn't keep up with your Jewish and secular studies, you would be kicked out. So school was just as challenging. I had problems paying attention in class. It always felt like the TV channel was changing in my head. I couldn't keep up, and then I was out. I bounced around from school to school to school, therapist's office to therapist's office. The answer at the time (hello, '90s!) was to "take some Ritalin and sit down." Eventually, I ended up on three other medications. The channel no longer felt like it was constantly changing, but the signal was just all static. I was such a vulnerable and open young man—just trying to fit in—but my connections with society back then taught me to close up. I feared the judgment and began to judge myself. (Special shout-out to Mrs. Dabah for her patience and actually *seeing* me. Dr. Goulet and Debbie Antar gave me a glimmer of hope, too.)

I had one safe place, though, where I felt some semblance of my true self—the kitchen. At the time, the Syrian Jewish community was still defined by traditional values. The men worked. The women made a beautiful home, and making that home began in the kitchen. The kitchen, and the powerful, strong women who inhabited it, saved me.

My Aunt Cheryl had a motto: "Be true to all of you." The kitchen was their sanctuary, the place where they were most themselves. They gossiped. They spoke of dreams and hopes for their families. Of their worries about their children. They shared stories of their own childhoods and made grocery lists. They cried; they laughed. They patted each other on the shoulder. They simmered sauces and rubbed ground allspice into lamb shanks with the same hands that so lovingly wiped tears from my face. It was their space, their own little community within a community. And they welcomed me into it with open arms—and a giant plate of food. (And if you were my Aunt Barbara, you'd offer me two plates of food. As she always said, "It wouldn't kill you to have leftovers"—so she cooked for an army.)

They may not have known what their welcoming did for me, but I watched them as they worked. My mother jokes that she liked having me there to "keep an eye on me," to stop me from causing too much trouble around the house. But I didn't mind. I was fascinated by the process, the food, and the scents that filled the air. And even if things got a bit messy, the end result was something beautiful and delicious. (It should be noted, however, that my mother keeps a *very* clean kitchen.)

My mother is blessed by the culinary gods—a truly gifted gourmet chef. If there were a term for having a green thumb in the kitchen, that would describe my mother. Without her, I wouldn't be the baker I am today. She knew her way around the kitchen, but, more importantly, she knew her way around a recipe. Recipes are often steeped in tradition and the occasional "family secret." My mother found a way to both keep the integrity of the recipe and put her mark on it—taking out the fat, but keeping the flavor—she's truly a master of the craft.

And I learned from my Grandma Peggy. On Thursday afternoons, I'd be with Grandma Peggy making challah. The goal was to make loaves to bring for Friday night Shabbat with the entire family. She wasn't just teaching me how to bake. I saw the braiding of the challah and learned that I could let my mind work through my hands. She could tell when I was stressed or frustrated, feeling the pressure of having to live up to the community's expectations and having to hide parts of myself in order to fit in. She'd tell me, "Jack, really put yourself into kneading this dough. Go deeper. The dough can take it." And it worked.

Grandma Peggy's kanafeh, with its rosewater scent, became synonymous with the sweetness of acceptance. And my Grandma Raquel's Guatamalan twist on traditional Syrian meals taught me how to blend who I am with where I come from. The aromas of all the family meals I watched these women cook comforted me. At the time, I didn't really have the proper tools to cope with the feeling of not belonging or the bullying. It wasn't easy. But these women helped form me. As I grew up in this hallowed space, I discovered something that I would not fully understand for years to come, something that began as a childhood sense of safety: baking as therapy.

I wouldn't truly come to understand Baking Therapy until I was already on my own, trying to forge my path in life. I was still part of a community, but I had to find my own way. I couldn't spend my life trying to fit into their idea of what life should be for me. I wanted—and still want—to have a family. Was I ever going to marry a woman? No. I kept getting fired from every job I ever held, so as a last resort, I went to work for the family business. Everyone knew it wasn't for me, and guess what? I caused myself to be fired. Again. It was yet another terrifying low point; hello, rock bottom!

My Aunt Dina, a social worker, inspired me to apply to NYU to become a licensed therapist. She reminded me that I was a bright spirit with a calling of my own. (Seriously, what would I do without the women in my life?) She knew I was good with people. And for me, I knew that I would always have a job.

I was still baking my famous challah every week. At the suggestion of my friend Murray's ex-girlfriend, I went to a Shabbat dinner one Friday at the Kabbalah Centre. Believe it or not, Madonna happened to be there. The Queen of Pop tried my challah—and loved it! "You, with the eyebrows. Did you make this?" I managed to stammer a "yes." That night gave me the confidence to start my JackBakes brand. Step aside, Madge, it's my time in the spotlight!

While studying to become a therapist, I sold my Madonna-approved challah for some extra income to help pay for rent. I had a lot to juggle: classes, making challah, an internship. But I had some time while the dough was rising to complete homework. Then it was back to hustling. And thanks to my Aunt Brenda, I was able to perfect the recipe for the masses. I became a second iteration of my grandfather, baking challah in a busted, old oven in an East Village studio apartment, hopping in my little Fiat 500, challah in the back, and knocking on doors at groceries. I didn't just want to get by in life. I wanted to manifest the life I knew I was meant for—to finally do something on my own terms.

Baking Is Therapy

Between the challah business and my psychology classes, I eventually arrived at a crossroads. I was struggling with choosing between the two; I loved, and wanted to pursue, both. But could I? Thankfully, I had another woman in my life to guide me: NYU professor Renee Exelbert. After I explained how I juggled everything through my three years and she tried some of my challah, she uttered the sweetest words: "Baking is therapy, Jack." Hello! Oven light moment! How could I have missed it?

Soon it came time to start my own therapy practice. It was "expected" that I engage in talk therapy, your standard therapy practice where you sit in chairs or on a couch and just talk. We all know how much I *love* tradition. (Insert eye roll.) Talk therapy hadn't worked when I was younger. At the end of each session, I felt like I didn't have the right tools to apply outside of the therapist's office. The world wasn't in therapy, I was. So, I couldn't, in good conscience, offer my patients that same experience. I wanted to give them guidance they could follow when we weren't together.

Look, starting therapy isn't easy. Being open and vulnerable can be more daunting than freeing for some. It's nearly impossible to open up to a stranger you've just met. Now you have to tell them your deepest, darkest secrets and fears? Talk about scary! I knew that my therapy practice had to be a welcoming environment for patients. It had to be true to me and helpful for my patients at the same time.

There was Professor Exelbert's voice in my head again: "Baking is therapy." I had flashes of my childhood days spent in the kitchen with the women in my family. Grandma Peggy and her baking techniques suddenly had more meaning. Baking created an outlet for nervous energy, quiet frustration, and even racing thoughts. It calmed my mind, the channels changing at a slower pace so I could enjoy what was on the screen.

And that, bakers, is how Baking Therapy got started! It would become part of the foundation of my practice, Modern Therapy Group, which offers up a different approach to traditional talk therapy.

I knew it was going to benefit my patients. Why? Because the kitchen is a safe space. Baking doesn't discriminate. It's something universal; every culture bakes. Everyone bakes, or has baked, at some point in their lives. And baking helped me through some of my darkest periods—and helped celebrate the bright ones.

Baking and this book are not meant to supplement or replace actual therapy. They're complementary. It doesn't matter what you're going through. You'll be able to express your feelings and emotions in a healthy and nonjudgmental space to just be you! And you'll be able to bring what you've learned in the kitchen into the real world, something I wish I had understood when I was younger, in and out of all those therapists' offices.

The beauty of Baking Therapy's universal approach is that everything is connected. But you'll see that the chapters in *Mind Over Batter* are very focused on central themes. Feeling frustrated? There's a chapter to work through it (page 166). Need some peace of mind? Check out Mindfulness (page 56) or Self-Care (page 22). My hope is that you're able to walk away with a connection between action and mindset. In other words, Baking Therapy is a healing process, broken down into bite-size, nourishing content. (See what I did there?)

Welcome to *Mind Over Batter,* bakers.

Warmly,
Jack

JUST A QUICK NOTE: *There are some things that baking can't fix that a licensed professional can help with. If you are in need, please find a therapist to speak to.*

Turning Your Kitchen into a Sanctuary

Before you get started on your baking therapy journey, let's talk about your kitchen—your safe space. A well-organized kitchen is just as important as what you're baking. If your kitchen is out of order, your life is out of order! I'm not saying you have to go full-on Marie Kondo and declutter or throw things out (though you should if they're expired). But I recommend turning your kitchen into a sanctuary, a calm place where you want to spend time, where you can embrace the lessons from this book. Here are a few ways to do that.

KNOW WHERE EVERYTHING IS. If you can't find a whisk, the sheet pans, or any of the ingredients you need, you won't be able to bake properly. So, try to create an organized system for your supplies. Place your wet and dry measuring cups together. Perhaps they go next to the gorgeous Pyrex bowls. The last thing you want is to be frantic in the kitchen; it's hard to create in chaos. Trust me on this, sweetie.

MISE EN PLACE. This French term means you have all your ingredients measured, cut, peeled, sliced, grated, etc. before you start baking. Your pans are prepared. Mixing bowls, tools, and equipment are set out. This is such an important part of preparing to bake, and why you need to know where everything is: so you can prepare and lay everything out in front of you. Your baking will go that much more smoothly for it.

HAVE PANTRY STAPLES AT THE READY. Most baking recipes call for flour, eggs, sugar, canola oil, etc. Having these pantry staples allows you to pop into the kitchen whenever the mood strikes. Without them, you now have to get in your car, drive to the store, hope they have what you need, and get back home to bake. If they don't? Ugh, your mood just got even worse. Stock up during your normal grocery run and save the additional trips to the store for more special ingredients like rose water. (Fun baking tip: You can swap avocado or coconut oil for canola oil for healthier and more elevated baking!)

OTHER STAPLES TO HAVE ON HAND

- Plastic wrap
- Parchment paper
- Wooden spoon
- Rubber spatula
- Pastry cutter
- Zester (we Syrian Jews love a good zesty moment)
- Piping bags and piping tips

PERSONALIZE YOUR SPACE. I've always found it a little bit tricky to bake in a new kitchen. I eventually find my way, but there's nothing quite like baking in a place that's "yours." I set my kitchen up with an Amazon Echo Show, allowing me to say, "Alexa, set the timer for twenty-five minutes," or to play music as I bake. Studies have shown the positive impact of music on our mood and experiences, but if you want silence as you bake, go for it. You can also put up pictures of friends or family. Or maybe you have little tchotchkes all around. The goal is to make your kitchen feel welcoming and warm to *you*!

TAKE CARE OF YOUR KITCHEN. Part of making your kitchen a place where you want to spend time is caring for it. If you don't clean up right after you cook, you're stuck staring at a stressful mess that no one wants to clean the next time you go to use the kitchen. Taking care of your kitchen takes care of you (and your mental health).

LEAVE DISTRACTIONS OUTSIDE. I'm probably the most guilty of this, but put the phone down! While you're baking, you do not need to check your email or pop-up notifications constantly. That "urgent" text can wait (and probably isn't really worth your energy anyway). Your baking time is precious—tune out the outside world and tune in to the recipe in front of you.

TAKE OWNERSHIP OF YOUR SPACE. You'll learn in the Connecting with Others chapter (page 200) how Baking Therapy can help with communication. Feel free to bring people into the kitchen to bake with you when it makes sense, but learn to leave them outside too. Once everything is baked and cooled, you can invite them to enjoy it with you. After all, you're setting yourself up to succeed in the kitchen, and part of that process is setting boundaries.

LET GO AND LET'S BAKE. These recipes are easy to follow, no matter your mastery in the kitchen. So have fun! If you want to experiment, go for it. Add more chocolate chips. Add some food coloring to the whipped cream. Lick the spoon. You might be working through some intense anger and pulverizing the cookies for that piecrust, so why not yell as you do it? (Try it. It's actually fun and sometimes really healthy to do.)

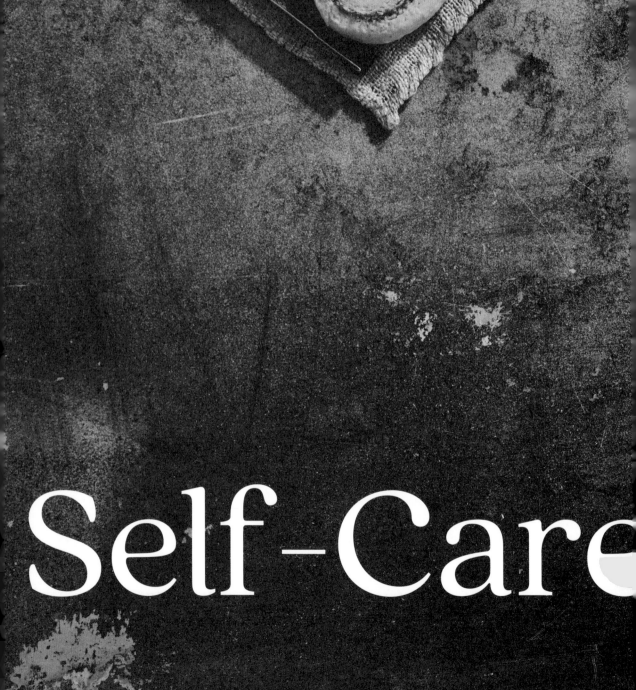

Self-Care

The term *self-care* is ubiquitous these days. Whether it's on Instagram, Pinterest, around the watercooler, you name it, everyone is talking about it. And everyone has their own definition for what self-care means to them. Most people just think of it as "full on pampering" like "taking time for yourself." We don't seem to dive deep into the abstract concepts of self-care, which means some of us don't really learn how to properly incorporate it into our lives.

The one thing that we all seem to agree on is that our society treats self-care as a luxury, not a necessity. Plant me in the middle of Italy or Spain and I will enjoy that afternoon siesta without the guilt trip. But when I'm home, back to the daily grind (the word *grind* makes my skin crawl; it's so tiring), I'm lucky if I take 20 minutes to rush through lunch. Spoiler alert: The moral of the story is make time to take care of yourself!

To explain it in psychology terms and not the fast-food version, it's about taking care of the *self*, the deeper *I*. I want you to imagine you're a car, driving around every day. At some point, the "check engine" light comes on. You ignore it; you're still driving smoothly and getting things done. But after a while, the gas tank starts to run low. Another warning light comes on. Suddenly, you're running on fumes, trying to get the same performance out of your car that you got in the beginning. The car will ultimately break down and stop working.

Long metaphor short, taking regular care of your car is going to help it function better in the long run. So, if you don't take care of yourself—regularly—your *self* is going to break. By the time you see the warning signs, things are already off the rails. Getting them back on track is going to take a lot of time and effort. (And a big hit to your wallet.)

Or look at it this way: We're all glued to our phones and freak out when the battery drops below 20 percent. Every app and every notification continue to drain the battery. And yet, somehow, we need our phone the most in that last 20 percent, when the battery seems to drain even more quickly. We give our phones a couple of hours to get the battery back up to 100 percent, so why aren't we doing the same thing with our minds and bodies?

That's why self-care is so important. You would benefit from becoming attuned to those moments when you have to fully unwind and recharge. You're not crazy, needy, or "unable to handle it all" because you're taking a self-care day. We all need a minute sometimes, so don't feel guilty for taking yours. You can't take care of others if you don't take care of yourself first.

Even as a therapist, I need my self-care moments too. When I'm swimming in a stream of creativity, my sessions have a really good flow to them. I'm showing up for my clients and providing them with the care they need. But even I hit a period when I was exhausted, mentally and emotionally, and the stream dried up. I was burnt out. I felt so trapped and I had to make a decision: sink or swim. So, with only a suitcase, I hopped on a one-way flight out of New York. "Give it six months," I told myself. It was the biggest leap I had ever taken. I had never left NYC for more than a week. Hell, I didn't move out of my parents' house until I was twenty-five. But I needed clarity that I wasn't getting in my city. I had to get out of my comfort zone if I was going to find actual comfort. Taking care of myself at that time would allow me to take care of my patients later.

I can't even call those six months a trip. They were a journey—to myself. It quieted the noise around me and inside my head so that I could hear my true self speak. (And in the city that never sleeps, trying to hear your inner voice can be really difficult.) I actually listened to what my *self* needed at that moment. I returned to NYC revitalized and ready to show up for life and others, in abundance!

Maybe moving to another city for six months isn't something you can do. But the goal here isn't to solely focus on external self-care, but to discover the things that make you feel good on the inside. I've come to realize that external changes are easier because we can see results faster (hello, instant gratification!), whereas internal self-care requires a lot of introspection.

It's like baking a beautifully decorated cake. If you choose to focus on creating a beautiful exterior, but it lacks the right flavors, what are you really left with? A cake that is crumbly, dry, unappetizing, flavorless . . . you get the idea. You have to care about what's on the inside in order to make the outside even more appetizing. That's why I believe in really good therapy. Good therapy will help you work through situations from the inside out.

Really good therapy can be expensive, no sugarcoating it. But therapy also isn't for everyone. So, find what works for you. You might be the type who recharges by going to the all-inclusive gym a few blocks away. You can also spend more time with your family, or take a night off from the usual and go to the movies or see a show. Baking Therapy is another fantastic way to explore your inner workings. One of my patients said to me, "So what you're saying is, 'I can't flourish if I don't nourish'?" (I admit, that was cute.) But yes! Baking Therapy not only provides the meditative qualities for self-care, but it also provides us with nourishment, filling our stomachs and souls with deliciousness.

As you go through this chapter, try to shut the outside world off and turn that oven on! Take an hour. Or two. These recipes are made for you to enjoy baking—and eating—by yourself. (If you want to share, I can't stop you, babe.) But as you bake, maybe use your phone only as a timer. Don't check for emails, text messages, or notifications. Set that boundary and stick to it.

One of my favorite recipes is the It's My Cookie and I'll Share If I Want To (page 49). Not only is it a gorgeous chocolate chip cookie to indulge in (hello ultimate self-care moment!), but it gives you the power to decide— a.k.a. creating a boundary—whether it's worth sharing. Talk about a win-win recipe!

Individually portioned baked goods are also perfect for a self-care moment. My Self-Care in a Cup Cake (page 35) is not meant to be shared! The beauty of this recipe isn't in the techniques, like so many of the others. This is that quick pick-me-up kind of treat. So grab that mug, curl up on the couch, and binge your latest TV obsession.

If you make it a ritual to find time for yourself in the kitchen baking (maybe every Sunday night to fight off the Sunday Scaries), you'll look forward to each Sunday trying a new recipe, biting into a sweet treat, and getting some self-care love—regularly. So, for those of you who need a good, reliable recipe to recharge, grab the mixer and start baking!

Quick Session
CREATE BOUNDARIES, NOT WALLS

The first step in taking care of yourself is learning how to set boundaries—not just with others (external) but also within yourself (internal). Both are important. They set up how you want to—no, should—be treated. Boundaries act as a mental, emotional, and sometimes physical force field to protect you for a hot minute. It teaches people how to treat us. If the threshold is passed, you walk away. A wall, on the other hand, is meant to keep people out (or lock them away if you're living in a fairy tale). Walls are unapproachable and can do more damage to our psyche than good.

I remind my clients that "no" is a complete sentence. If they tell someone no, it should be respected—no matter the situation. You cannot bend and snap (no, not the Elle Woods kind) for everyone and expect not to break at some point. So, teach people how to treat you.

One of my patients was a high-profile executive who struggled with creating boundaries. At work, he was in high demand; everyone was always taking something from him—his time, advice, you name it. When he got home, the high demand intensified between the wife and the kids. He was so used to catering to others that he wasn't catering to himself. The perpetual cycle started to impact his job, his home life, and his inner self. With that in mind, I challenged him with some Baking Therapy homework.

His assignment was to bake with his kids—no phone, no distractions. Just them in the kitchen. "But, work . . ." No. (See, it works!) Work can wait. Emails can wait. Shut the phone off and focus on being present. If spending time with loved ones is what really brings you happiness and meaning, then make sure you savor the time with them. Work will still be there when it's over.

The result? Work continued. Nothing crashed and burned, as he envisioned happening. The kids enjoyed time with their dad. And he finally felt like himself again. I can't tell you his name, but he definitely got his groove back.

BOUNDARY EXERCISE:

Write a list of boundaries, or non-negotiables, of what you're willing or unwilling to accept from others—or yourself.

Better Than Sex Cake

CAKE

2 Tbsp unsweetened cocoa powder

4 cups [480 g] devil's food cake mix (use your favorite boxed mix!)

¾ cup [180 g] sour cream

½ cup [120 ml] canola oil

¼ cup [30 g] vanilla pudding mix

1½ cups [270 g] semisweet chocolate chips

¾ cup [90 g] chopped pecans

CHOCOLATE GANACHE

1 cup [180 g] chopped, high-quality semisweet chocolate

¾ cup [180 ml] heavy cream

CARAMEL BUTTERCREAM

1 cup [220 g] unsalted butter, at room temperature

⅓ cup [155 g] Caramel Sauce (recipe follows)

2 cups [240 g] powdered sugar

MAKES 8 SLICES

My Grandma Peggy always said, "Taste it. If it's sexless, add more flavor!" Well, this cake has that in spades—with caramel buttercream and chocolate ganache—so indulge yourself. Physical intimacy can be important for mental well-being, but you shouldn't always rely on someone else to take care of your needs. Baking can be a less complicated way to care for ourselves that doesn't require validation from others.

TO MAKE THE CAKE:

1. Preheat the oven to 350°F [180°C] and grease three 8 in [20 cm] cake pans with 2 Tbsp of shortening. Sprinkle the cocoa powder onto the cake pans in an even layer to coat the inside. Shake off any excess cocoa and set the pans aside.

2. In a large bowl, combine the cake mix, sour cream, oil, and vanilla pudding mix with 2 cups [480 ml] of water and mix until just combined. Fold in the chocolate chips and pecans. This cake is very forgiving and fun, so don't stress about how long you mix. It will work out no matter what!

3. Pour the batter evenly into the prepared pans and bake for 20 to 30 minutes, or until a toothpick inserted into the centers comes out with just a few crumbs. Set the pans aside on cooling racks.

NOTE: *Make sure your bowl is completely dry. Any amount of water will make the chocolate seize. I learned this the hard way by ruining 20 lb [9.1 kg] of imported Swiss chocolate.*

BAKING AFFIRMATION:
Today I make a commitment to give myself what I need, whether it's for my entire self, or just a part of me.

TO MAKE THE GANACHE:

1. Combine the chocolate and cream in a dry microwave-safe bowl (see Note). Microwave on low for 30 seconds. Stir and repeat until the chocolate is completely melted. You do not want the cream to boil, so be sure to watch it carefully. Once the chocolate is melted, keep stirring until a thick and creamy ganache forms. Place in the fridge to cool for a thick ganache that can be piped, or simply set aside to cool at room temperature for a pourable ganache.

TO MAKE THE BUTTERCREAM:

1. In the bowl of a stand mixer fitted with the paddle attachment, or in a medium bowl using a handheld electric mixer, beat the butter and caramel sauce until fluffy. Add 1 cup [120 g] of the powdered sugar and beat on low speed until combined, and then add the remaining 1 cup [120 g] of powdered sugar. Turn your mixer up to medium-high and beat the buttercream until it becomes light and fluffy, using a spatula to scrape down the sides. Cover the bowl with plastic wrap and set it aside in the fridge until ready to use.

TO ASSEMBLE AND DECORATE THE CAKES:

1. Once the cakes have cooled, gather all your pent-up emotions and get ready to slam some pans around. Take a cake pan in your hands, quickly flip it upside down, and slam it cake-side down onto the counter. You heard right. These cakes are so decadent and dense that they need some serious urging to leave the pans sometimes. Repeat this process with the remaining cakes.

cont.

2.	Using a serrated knife, shave off the top layer of each cake so that they are level and even. You can discard the cake tops or eat them while you decorate. That's what I do.

3.	This is where you get to be creative. You can use the ganache or buttercream to layer your cakes. You can use them as the outer icing. You can use them for both! I like to use the buttercream to layer my cakes, then cover the outer layer with the ganache and top it with alternating rosettes of caramel butter-cream and chilled ganache. You can't do it wrong, so explore! Serve immediately or store tightly wrapped in plastic wrap at room temperature for 2 to 3 days.

Caramel Sauce

MAKES 1½ CUPS [700 G]

This recipe is time-sensitive, so mise en place is an important first step. Set out all of your ingredients within reach of your stove top.

1 cup [200 g] sugar

¾ cup [180 ml] heavy cream, at room temperature

2 Tbsp salted butter, at room temperature

1 tsp vanilla extract

1.	Gently pour the sugar into a completely dry 4 qt [3.8 L] saucepan. Gently pour ⅓ cup [80 ml] of warm water over the sugar. Your goal is to make sure no water splashes up the sides of the pan, as this can cause the caramel to crystalize. Grab your drink of choice and get ready to watch a pot boil because you can't leave again until the caramel is done (don't worry, it's only about 10 minutes).

2. Turn the heat to medium and allow the sugar mixture to boil. Do not stir or move the pan at all. The sugar will dissolve into a clear syrup. At this point, turn the heat up just a smidge and watch the sugar like a hawk. It will begin to take on a golden color.

3. Once the caramel has turned to a light amber color, turn off the heat and slowly pour in the heavy cream. Immediately add the butter and whisk the ingredients together. The caramel will likely seize up at this point, but don't worry. Keep whisking and it should all melt together quite nicely within a few moments.

4. Once the caramel is mostly smooth, add the vanilla. Place a fine-mesh sieve over a microwave-safe bowl or jar and pour the caramel through it so that any crystallized sugar is removed, being careful while pouring because the mixture will be quite hot.

5. You now have a jar of delicious homemade caramel sauce. Show it off to all your friends because it's that much better than store-bought.

Self-Care in a Cup Cake

¼ cup [35 g] all-purpose flour

1 Tbsp packed brown sugar

¼ tsp baking powder

¼ tsp ground cinnamon

⅛ tsp ground allspice

3 Tbsp half-and-half

1 Tbsp salted butter, melted

¼ tsp vanilla extract

1 Tbsp maple syrup

SERVES 1

I created this recipe when I was craving something sweet but just didn't have the energy for a real bake. And then, I made it again. And again. I ate this bad boy four nights in a row. (Don't judge me.) Sometimes, we get so exhausted by our daily lives that we need a little pick-me-up at the end of a long day or week. This cake is so simple and uses only ingredients you're sure to have sitting in your pantry. You'll have plenty of time to make your dessert and eat it too. The best part is that cleanup is just a mug and spoon.

1. In a 12 oz [360 ml] mug, use a fork to whisk together the flour, brown sugar, baking powder, cinnamon, and allspice. Add the half-and-half, butter, and vanilla and stir until the batter just comes together.

2. Microwave the mug mixture for 60 seconds, or until the cake just begins to pull away from the sides of the mug. Let the cake sit for 2 minutes, as it will be very hot.

3. Top the cake with the maple syrup, grab a spoon, and dig in!

FOOD FOR THOUGHT:
It's important to make self-care part of your routine, even when your life seems completely outrageous. Be sure to take little moments for yourself, even if it's just for a bite of cake!

Boost-of-Energy Coconut Lime Bites

1 cup [140 g] unsalted roasted cashews

2 Tbsp ground flaxseed

1 Tbsp chia seeds

1 tsp ground turmeric

1 cup [180 g] packed, pitted dates

3 Tbsp fresh lime juice

1 cup [80 g] unsweetened shredded coconut

MAKES 10 TO 12 BITES

We can all use a little boost every now and then. We so often run ourselves ragged and drain ourselves of our precious energy. These energy bites are a sweet little pick-me-up that you can prep on Sunday and have ready all through the week! With ingredients that are super good for you, like coconut, flaxseed, and turmeric, these deca-dent bites give you a kick in a way that respects your body and keeps your health in mind.

1. In a food processor, pulse the cashews until coarsely ground. Add the flaxseed, chia seeds, and turmeric and pulse for 10 seconds to combine.

2. Next, add the dates and lime juice to the food pro-cessor and pulse until a sticky mixture forms. Add the shredded coconut and pulse until well combined.

3. Scoop the mixture into a small bowl. Shape about 2 Tbsp into a ball. Continue until all the mixture is gone.

4. Refrigerate the bites for at least 1 hour in a sealed container. Enjoy them as a quick snack whenever the need strikes. Keep the bites in a sealed container in the fridge for up to 5 days.

FOOD FOR THOUGHT:
What do you need right now to feel recharged or revived?

Peanut Butter Pretzel Pie

CRUST

1½ cups [100 g] finely chopped hard pretzels

6 Tbsp [85 g] unsalted butter, melted

1 egg, lightly beaten

FILLING

1 cup [260 g] creamy peanut butter

8 oz [230 g] cream cheese, at room temperature

1 cup [120 g] powdered sugar

½ cup [50 g] marshmallow creme

1 cup [115 g] Homemade Whipped Cream (recipe follows)

GARNISH

1 cup [100 g] marshmallow creme

1 recipe Chocolate Ganache (page 30)

SERVES 8

Dare I say it: Baking can be complicated. I'm pleased to report that this pie only looks like a complicated confection—it's actually so easy to make! Allow yourself to get lost in crushing the pretzels or whipping the peanut butter. Remember: This doesn't have to be "perfect," but it will be delicious. With the uncertainty of the world around us, taking on a new task can sometimes feel daunting. You really can't mess up this recipe, so this is a great project to help you feel safe while trying something new.

TO MAKE THE CRUST:

1. Preheat the oven to 350°F [180°C].

2. In a medium bowl, combine the pretzel pieces, butter, and egg. Press the mixture on the bottom and sides of a 9 in [23 cm] pie pan. Bake for 7 minutes, then set aside to cool.

TO MAKE THE FILLING:

1. In the bowl of a stand mixer fitted with the paddle attachment, or in a medium bowl using a handheld electric mixer, beat the peanut butter, cream cheese, and powdered sugar on low speed until smooth. Add the marshmallow creme and continue to mix until well incorporated. Add the whipped cream and mix gently until just combined and smooth. You don't want to overmix at this point, as it will deflate the whipped cream.

2. Use a spatula to evenly spread the pie filling into the prepared crust. Refrigerate the pie for at least 1 hour or overnight.

TO GARNISH THE PIE:

1. Remove the pie from the fridge. Fit a piping bag with a round tip and fill with the marshmallow creme, then pipe it onto the pie filling. The pressure of pushing the fluff through the piping tip will make it lose its shape and take on a melty appearance. This is what you want because it allows you to cover the top in marshmallow creme without making a mess of the pie filling.

2. Next, fill a clean piping bag with the chocolate ganache and drizzle chocolate over the top of the marshmallow creme. Feel free to get a little wild with it! Refrigerate until ready to serve. Store leftovers in the fridge for up to 3 days.

Homemade Whipped Cream
MAKES 1 CUP [115 G]

½ cup [120 ml] heavy cream, very cold

2 Tbsp powdered sugar

¼ tsp vanilla extract

⅛ tsp rose water or orange blossom water (optional)

Most people wouldn't think to make whipped cream at home, but that's because they don't realize how easy it is! Feel free to add rose water or orange blossom water—it gives it a little extra zhuzh—for special events or desserts. Also, eat a spoonful right out of the bowl. You deserve it.

cont.

NOTE: *Be careful not to overwhip the cream, or you will essentially end up with a yellowed, buttery mixture. Mix just until stiff peaks begin to form. If you store the whipped cream for later use, bring out the mixer to re-fluff it for a minute before serving.*

1. Place a large metal bowl in the freezer for at least 10 minutes. The colder it is, the better the whipped cream will stand.

2. Add the heavy cream, powdered sugar, vanilla, and rose water (if using) to the cold bowl. Use a handheld mixer or whisk (if you are feeling extra tough today) to whip the cream until stiff peaks form. If using a handheld mixer, use a whisk attachment and start on low speed, moving to high speed as the cream begins to thicken.

3. Use the whipped cream immediately or store it in an airtight container in the fridge for up to 3 days.

BAKING AFFIRMATION:
I am making a conscious effort to not judge myself, especially not in the kitchen.

Slice-and-Bake Raspberry Pecan Cookies

DOUGH

1 cup [220 g] unsalted butter, at room temperature

1 cup [200 g] granulated sugar

½ cup [100 g] packed light brown sugar

½ tsp baking powder

½ tsp table salt

2 eggs

3½ cups [490 g] all-purpose flour

FILLING

1 cup [120 g] fresh raspberries

1 cup [140 g] pecans

¼ cup [50 g] packed light brown sugar

1 tsp ground cinnamon

¼ tsp ground nutmeg

MAKES 36 COOKIES

You know those rolls of sugar cookie dough that taunt you from the grocery store shelf? Kiss them goodbye. These cookies elevate that boring cookie dough and freeze so well that they'll always be available for your future self. Just preheat your oven, slice, and bake.

TO MAKE THE DOUGH:

1. In the bowl of a stand mixer fitted with the paddle attachment, or in a medium bowl using a handheld electric mixer, cream the butter, granulated sugar, and light brown sugar until fluffy. Add the baking powder, salt, and eggs, and continue mixing on low speed for about 1 minute. Add the flour, 1 cup [140 g] at a time, mixing continuously and scraping down the sides of the bowl with a rubber spatula as needed. Cover the bowl with plastic wrap and refrigerate for 2 hours or overnight.

TO MAKE THE FILLING:

1. Put the raspberries, pecans, brown sugar, cinnamon, and nutmeg in a food processor. Pulse until combined; do not turn it into a paste. If you do not have a food processor, chop the pecans finely, mash the raspberries, and mix them with the remaining ingredients. Set the filling aside.

TO ASSEMBLE AND BAKE:

1. Once the dough is thoroughly chilled, lay two large pieces of wax paper on your work surface. Divide the

cont.

dough in half, and cover and refrigerate the half you aren't using. Place the other half between the wax paper sheets. Use a rolling pin to roll the dough into a rectangle about 12 by 6 in [30.5 by 15 cm] and ¼ in [6 mm] thick.

2. Remove the top layer of wax paper and use a spatula to evenly spread half of the filling over the surface of the cookie dough. Be sure to leave a small margin on all sides. Roll the dough into a log, starting with one of the short ends and discarding the bottom wax paper as you roll. If the dough is too sticky, use the sharp edge of a long knife to help it get started. Cut off ½ in [13 mm] from each end of the log.

3. Wrap the dough tightly in wax paper and tie it off or tape it closed. Repeat these steps with the remaining dough and filling. Allow them to chill in the fridge for at least 12 hours.

4. At this point, you can freeze the dough or bake it fresh. When you're ready to bake, preheat the oven to 375°F [190°C]. Remove the dough from its wrapping and slice into ¼ in [6 mm] thick cookies. Place the cookies on a nonstick baking sheet and bake for 12 to 14 minutes, until the edges are set. (If baking from frozen, bake for 20 minutes.) The cookies can easily overbake, so pull them out even if they look underdone. Allow the cookies to cool on the baking sheet for 5 minutes before transferring to a cooling rack.

5. The dough will keep, tightly wrapped in the freezer, for up to 3 months.

Tahini Blondies

WITH BLACK AND WHITE SESAME SEEDS

1¼ cups [175 g] all-purpose flour

1 tsp baking powder

½ tsp fine sea salt

¼ tsp ground cinnamon

¼ tsp ground cardamom

2 tsp black sesame seeds

2 tsp white sesame seeds

1 tsp flaky sea salt (optional)

½ cup [120 ml] vegetable oil

1½ cups [300 g] packed
light brown sugar

1 large egg plus 1 large egg yolk

1 cup [220 g] tahini

1½ tsp vanilla extract

BAKING AFFIRMATION:
I have earned the right to this
bite. I don't need a reason to
treat myself.

MAKES 16 BLONDIES

Tahini is rich in healthy fats, antioxidants, and vitamins, making it easy to take care of your body and your soul at the same time. No wonder Syrians love tahini!

1. Preheat the oven to 350°F [180°C]. Butter an 8 in [20 cm] square baking pan or spray with nonstick cooking spray, line it with parchment paper, leaving enough of an overhang to help lift out the cooled blondies, and butter the parchment.

2. In a large bowl, sift together the flour, baking powder, fine sea salt, cinnamon, and cardamom. In a small bowl, mix together the black and white sesame seeds with the flaky sea salt (if using) and set aside.

3. In a medium bowl, whisk together the vegetable oil and brown sugar. Add the egg and egg yolk and mix thoroughly. Add the tahini and vanilla and mix again. Fold the wet mixture into the flour mixture and mix gently until just combined.

4. Pour the batter into the prepared pan, smooth the top with an offset spatula, and top with the sesame seed mixture. Bake for 24 to 26 minutes, or until golden brown on the edges and baked through in the middle. Let cool in the pan on a wire rack for 2 hours.

5. Cut into sixteen squares. Store in an airtight container at room temperature for up to 3 days or in the freezer for up to 30 days.

Mushroom and Gruyère Quiche (WITH GLUTEN-FREE VARIATION)

CRUST

3 cups [420 g] all-purpose flour

1 cup [226 g] salted butter, very cold, cut into cubes

½ cup [120 ml] plus 2 Tbsp whole milk

GLUTEN-FREE CRUST VARIATION

3 cups [420 g] gluten-free all-purpose flour

2 tsp xantham gum

1 cup [226 g] salted butter, very cold, cut into cubes

½ cup [120 ml] plus 2 Tbsp whole milk

FILLING

1 Tbsp olive oil

2 lb [910 g] baby bella mushrooms, cleaned and sliced

2 sprigs fresh thyme, leaves stripped and chopped

1 sprig fresh rosemary, leaves stripped and chopped

2 garlic cloves, minced

1 cup [20 g] fresh spinach

cont.

SERVES 8

Savory baking is so often overlooked, but this quiche will change all of that. Vegetarian, with an easy gluten-free variation, it's the perfect dish to bring to a brunch. With hearty mushrooms, tender spinach, and fresh herbs, this quiche will satisfy everyone at the table and give them some nutrients too!

TO MAKE THE CRUST:

1. In a large bowl, whisk together the flour and xantham gum (if doing the gluten-free variation). Add the butter and use a pastry cutter or two forks to cut it into the flour until sandy crumbs form. Add the milk and use a large spoon or rubber spatula to work the mixture into a dough. Once the dough comes together, use your hands to finish mixing the dough and form it into a 1 in [2.5 cm] thick disk. Wrap the dough in plastic wrap and refrigerate for at least 20 minutes and up to 2 hours.

TO MAKE THE FILLING:

1. While the dough chills, heat the olive oil in a skillet over medium heat and add the mushrooms, thyme, and rosemary. Sauté until the mushrooms are cooked through and have released most of their moisture, about 7 minutes. Add the garlic and spinach and sauté for an additional 30 seconds. Transfer the mixture to a bowl. Add the green onions, cheeses, eggs, milk, heavy cream, and pepper to the bowl and stir to combine well. Set aside.

cont.

½ bunch green onions, chopped

1 cup [80 g] shredded
Gruyère cheese

⅓ cup [10 g] shredded
Parmesan cheese

4 eggs, beaten

1 cup [240 ml] whole milk

1 cup [240 ml] heavy cream

¼ tsp freshly ground black pepper

NOTE: *If you can't find Gruyère,
shredded mozzarella will work
as well.*

FOOD FOR THOUGHT:
Being good to yourself means
nourishing your body as well as
your mind.

TO ASSEMBLE AND BAKE THE QUICHE:

1. Preheat the oven to 400°F [200°C]. Have a 9 in
   [23 cm] deep-dish pie dish ready.

2. Using a sprinkling of the flour or gluten-free flour,
   flour your work surface and a rolling pin. Feel free
   to be liberal with the flour here, as you can always
   dust off the excess. Roll the dough out into a 12 in
   [30.5 cm] circle. Use your rolling pin to transfer the
   crust to the pie dish. Trim the extra dough from the
   edges and patch any cracks or tears. Use the tines of
   a fork or your fingers to crimp the edges of the crust
   into a pattern. Use a fork to poke several holes in the
   bottom of the pie crust. This will help prevent it from
   bubbling up.

3. Line the crust with parchment paper and fill it with
   pie weights (uncooked rice or dry beans also work
   great) and bake for 15 minutes. Remove the crust
   from the oven, remove the weights, and discard
   the parchment paper. Lower the oven temperature
   to 350°F [180°C].

4. Pour the filling into the par-baked crust. Place the
   pie dish on a baking sheet to catch any drips. Bake,
   uncovered, for 30 minutes, then cover the entire top
   with aluminum foil. Bake for another 30 minutes, or
   until set. When you lightly jiggle the dish, the center
   should be just set. If it still wobbles, it needs more time.

5. Remove the quiche from the oven and allow to cool
   for at least 20 minutes before serving. Store leftovers
   in the fridge for up to 3 days.

It's My Cookie and I'll Share If I Want To

¾ cup [165 g] unsalted butter

½ cup [100 g] granulated sugar

½ cup [100 g] packed light brown sugar

¼ cup [50 g] packed dark brown sugar

1 Tbsp vanilla extract

1 tsp fine sea salt

1 egg, plus 1 large egg yolk

1¾ cups [245 g] all-purpose flour

½ tsp baking soda

1 cup [180 g] chocolate chunks or chips

SERVES 6

Technically this is only one cookie—one big, gooey, chocolate chip cookie. And it's easy to make! Part of feeling good and taking care of yourself is supersizing something you already love. So, forget about portion control for a minute. Indulge yourself!

1. Preheat the oven to 350°F [180°C].

2. Melt ½ cup [110 g] of the butter in a 9 in [23 cm] cast-iron skillet over medium-low heat. Stir frequently; the butter will foam and bubble and then get tan flecks in it. The whole process takes about 5 minutes, so don't walk away, as it can burn easily. Carefully transfer the warm browned butter to a large bowl and stir in the remaining ¼ cup [55 g] of cold butter until it is all completely melted. Set the now-empty skillet aside but don't wash it.

3. Add the granulated sugar, light brown sugar, dark brown sugar, vanilla, and salt to the butter and whisk to combine. Add the egg and yolk and mix thoroughly.

4. Stir together the flour and baking soda in a small bowl and then add it to the wet mixture.

5. Chop ¾ cup [135 g] of the chocolate and add it to the dough. Feel free to chop the chocolate into big or small pieces—or a mix of both to give each bite its own unique texture. Transfer the dough to the cast-iron skillet and smooth the top with an offset spatula.

cont.

NOTE: *A cast-iron skillet creates a great crust on the cookie. Please, please, please, use a pot holder when you are lifting and moving the cast-iron skillet; the handle gets super hot on the stove top. If you don't have a cast-iron skillet, use an oven-safe nonstick frying pan. It works just as well.*

Top with the remaining ¼ cup [45 g] of whole chocolate chunks or chips.

6.   Bake for 20 minutes, or until the top is golden brown. Place on a cooling rack for 30 minutes, then cut into wedges and serve. The leftovers can be stored in an airtight container for 3 days at room temperature or for 2 months in the freezer.

BAKING AFFIRMATION:
Investing in my "self" is the best investment I can make.

Individual Baked Apples

WITH CRUMBLE TOPPING

5 large apples (my favorites are Granny Smith, Fuji, Pink Lady, or Honeycrisp)

⅓ cup [65 g] packed light brown sugar

¼ cup [35 g] all-purpose flour

2 Tbsp unsalted butter, at room temperature

Pinch of fine sea salt

¼ cup [30 g] chopped nuts (I like walnuts)

2 Tbsp honey

½ tsp ground cinnamon

½ tsp vanilla extract

2 tsp granulated sugar

Ice cream, Homemade Whipped Cream (page 39), or Cheater Crème Anglaise (recipe follows) for serving

SERVES 4

Some days you feel like your life is crumbling around you; pieces of you keep being taken by coworkers, friends, even your family. I'll admit, it can be hard to keep it all together. But this recipe is perfect for when you need a little me time: An apple a day keeps the blues away! The crumble topping comes together to create a beautifully textured bite, reminding you that life is sweet—even if it doesn't look it.

1. Preheat the oven to 375°F [190°C].

2. Take four of the apples and cut about ½ in [13 mm] off the top of each. Scoop the entire insides out (mostly seeds and stem), being careful not to break the skin or cut through the bottom layer. Discard the insides.

3. In a medium bowl, combine the brown sugar, flour, butter, and sea salt with your hands (or two forks) until a crumbly mixture forms. Set the crumb mixture aside.

4. Peel and core the remaining apple and chop the flesh into tiny cubes. Put them in a medium bowl and stir in the nuts, honey, cinnamon, and vanilla. Stuff this mixture into the cored apples and top them with the crumb topping. Leave a small border so you can see where the chopped apples are and determine when they're done baking. Sprinkle the tops with the granulated sugar.

cont.

5. Place the apples in a pie plate and fill the bottom with 1 in [2.5 cm] of water. Cover tightly with aluminum foil and bake for 20 minutes. Carefully remove the foil and bake for another 20 minutes, or until the apples are tender. Let cool for 5 minutes, then serve with ice cream.

Cheater Crème Anglaise

8 oz [230 g] premium vanilla ice cream (I like Häagen-Dazs here)

1. Place the ice cream in a bowl. Let it melt to a liquid state and stir. That's it!

FOOD FOR THOUGHT:
You can't pour from an empty vessel. Today, put yourself at the top of the list.

Eat-All-You-Want Edible Cookie Dough

1¼ cups [175 g] all-purpose flour

½ tsp kosher salt

¼ tsp ground cinnamon

½ cup [110 g] vegan butter substitute, at room temperature

¾ cup [150 g] packed light brown sugar

¼ cup [50 g] granulated sugar

1 tsp vanilla extract

1 to 2 Tbsp nondairy milk of your choice (optional)

1 cup [180 g] vegan chocolate chips

SERVES 8 (OR 1 HUNGRY PERSON)

Sometimes you just need a direct container-to-mouth cookie experience for those days when even turning on the oven can feel daunting. And this tasty, creamy, vegan, no-bake cookie dough has you covered. So go ahead—indulge! It's (almost) good for you.

1. Preheat the oven to 350°F [180°C]. Line a rimmed baking sheet with parchment paper.

2. Spread the flour onto the parchment-lined baking sheet and bake for 6 to 7 minutes, or until the flour reads at least 165°F [75°C] with an instant-read thermometer. Allow to cool completely, then mix in the salt and cinnamon.

3. In a stand mixer with a paddle attachment or a large bowl with a handheld electric mixer, cream the vegan butter, light brown sugar, and granulated sugar at medium speed until light and fluffy. Add the vanilla, then beat the mixture again to incorporate.

4. Add in the heat-treated flour mixture and beat until just combined; if the mixture is still too dry and crumbly, add 1 to 2 Tbsp nondairy milk until it comes together. Fold in the vegan chocolate chips with a silicone spatula.

5. Store in an airtight container in the fridge for up to 4 days. Feel free to roll into 1 in [2.5 cm] balls or use a spoon to scoop when serving.

BAKING AFFIRMATION:
Asking for help or taking a break is not a sign of weakness. It's a sign of caring about my needs.

M

A full mind cannot be mindful.

Mindfulness is "being aware" of what you're feeling, thinking, and experiencing—acknowledging all of it. It's not about being overly reactive or overwhelmed. Don't rock the boat to create more waves! Try to steady yourself so you can see what's in front of you.

"Mindfulness" may seem like another word du jour—like the latest self-help fad—but it's actually one of the most important concepts to understand for better mental health (read: decluttering the mind). It's why yoga and meditation are worldwide phenomenons—we're all trying to find our inner peace to center ourselves. And like anything worth doing, it's one of the hardest things to truly master. (Believe me, I know. Mr. ADHD over here. It's like a love affair with distractions in my mind at all times.)

The good news? There are many simple ways to calm the mind (from anywhere, really) when distractions keep us from being fully present in our lives. But before we can make any meaningful, lasting change, we first have to understand why our minds are so full that we cannot calm them. I believe it's a commitment to the moment. It's recognizing that the sum is greater than its parts (more on this later).

First, let's try to rid ourselves of our distractions or our judgments of a situation. Is the restaurant taking *forever* to bring the food out? Remain calm. Did the waiter screw up the order? Take a deep breath. The more we end up judging outward onto others, the less mindful we become—and the less fun we have in the process (insert that side-eye from my friends when I inevitably speak up).

We also want to be mindful that we're not trying to *escape* a situation but instead *embrace* it. Have you ever been on a date where you're trying to hatch an escape plan every five minutes? Here's a perfectly cute person trying to engage, and you're just not having it. You're checking your phone or making an excuse to go to the bathroom. Whatever it is, you're not being present and mindful of the date. And it sucks when you're on the receiving end of the same actions.

The worst distractions appear at the most unfortunate, and often random, times. Did you remember to turn off the stove? Is your curling iron still on? Is that cute boy from the bar going to text you back? Honey, the list can go on and on. In those moments, you totally missed out on your friend's incredible story. Or the project your boss just asked you to work on.

Not all distractions are "bad." As someone who used to doodle all the time during class, I actually retain information better when my hands are busy. Doodling keeps my brain more focused by keeping my otherwise-distracted-self occupied. And when I found baking, it provided some of the same meditative, focusing qualities that doodling did.

Lack of mindfulness can lead to an incredibly frantic mind. One of the worst baking experiences I've ever had happened while not being mindful in the moment. Growing up, I was always asked to make desserts for holiday meals—a role I usually accepted with pleasure. However, this one holiday I was having a very chaotic day, frantically running all over. I wasn't in my right mind.

I decided to make this delicious chocolate cake I had made a dozen times. I knew the recipe by heart. I was so proud of myself when it was served— but then my ego was instantly bruised. My family took one bite and began coughing and retching from it! (AAH!) My mom rushed to the kitchen to grab a glass of water. I couldn't understand why they were being so rude . . . until I tasted my cake.

My distracted mind had carried over into the kitchen. The first bite gave me a brief moment of clarity; I realized that I had put coarse kosher salt into the batter instead of sugar. That's not even a rookie mistake! I had essentially ruined dessert that night, not to mention everyone's taste buds for a good five minutes. Looking back at that night, my family laughs about it. But it's still mortifying.

The lesson? Baking is all about precision. Try to remain calm and present as you bake. If you don't, it'll come back to bite you in the butt.

Baking can be a very mindful experience. Sure, you can use an app to meditate and focus on your breathing, but you can also jump into the kitchen. Baking engages each of our senses and helps calm our minds. Take the Summer Fruit Crumble (page 66), for example. The sight of the vibrant fruit, the sound of the knife chopping, the texture of the brown sugar and cinnamon-oat crumble, the delightful aroma as it bakes, and that first sweet bite all play a role in focusing our senses to be present in that activity.

But we can't appreciate the full, meditative experience if we're not being mindful. "Busy baking," a term I just coined, leads to unfavorable results, like my cake fiasco (and yes, I'm still salty about that—pun intended). It's essentially mindless baking: You're going through the motions, but you're not paying attention to what you're actually doing. How else did the eggshell end up in the batter, hun? So, if you're going to bake, bake. As in life, it's not something you can just half-ass and expect to turn out perfect.

Perfection: It's overrated! And worrying about it is another way to pull yourself out of your mindful space. When you're learning a new skill, like baking, often your inner critic comes out to play. "Am I doing this right?" "Is this flavor profile going to be amazing?" "Oh no, that last icing did not pipe evenly." The constant reassessment and second-guessing is your brain's way of trying to control the situation. But the thing is, no one else is going to notice. They're going to see a beautifully decorated, delicious cake. So don't try to control every little piece. Ignoring that inner critic is beneficial to your mindfulness.

It reminds me of the Great Raisin lesson my NYU professor, Dr. Renee Exelbert, taught in grad school. She passed out a raisin to each student, and asked us to examine it, to feel the wrinkles and the depressions on the exterior. Then, we popped it into our mouths. With a slight chew, we tasted its sweetness. We felt its tenderness. From the outside, it looked less than perfect. But it was enjoyable to eat.

At the end of the day, don't overthink it! Baking Therapy is here to help you feel more connected to what you're making, helping to calm your mind and be more conscious in your actions.

A QUICK BAKING MEDITATION

- Step 1: Take a deep breath, hold, and release (repeating three times should do the trick).

- Step 2: Speak your intention out loud. Why are you baking today? What are you baking?

- Step 3: Let go. Free yourself from feeling overwhelmed by the process and take it one step at a time.

- Step 4: Have fun!

Quick Session

NINE WAYS TO FIND MINDFULNESS IN BAKING

My practice is based in New York, and any New Yorker will tell you that the city never sleeps, which means you're always on. Finding a way to shut that off is one reason patients come to see me. In turn, I offer up mindfulness techniques for clients to calm down and center themselves.

I open up the session with a body scan check-in. According to the father of mindfulness, expert Jon Kabat-Zinn, this act is about befriending the body, from the soles of your feet to the top of your head. I ask my patients if they can feel—or recognize—the big toe versus the pinky toe. I ask them to find the area that feels tension and "release it." This is something they can easily do at home.

Kabat-Zinn also developed nine key principles for finding mindfulness. When I share these with my patients, I like to connect it to things they can understand: being in the kitchen and baking.

1.   **LETTING GO:** A perfectly baked treat doesn't exist! Once we place the batter in the oven, we should let go of the outcome and remind ourselves of the effort we put in. In other words, appreciate the result, however it turns out.

2.   **GENEROSITY:** Give with no expectation of anything in return, or what's in it for you. One way to do that is to bake something sweet and share it with someone. My mother would spend every Friday prepping a gourmet Shabbat meal for us. She knew it was important to focus on the upcoming meal so her family would be well fed with her culinary prowess.

3.   **NONJUDGING:** We are quick to judge (even that was judgy). When it comes to baking, we can take a moment to acknowledge our inner critic and use the opportunity to distance ourselves from it. So go ahead and get a little messy. Even more

important, don't hold yourself to some perfect standard. Go easy on yourself.

4. **ACCEPTANCE:** Lose the idea that it's either "your way or the highway." We'd all love for something or someone to be a certain way, but the real power is in accepting a situation for what it is. Can you accept that the final dish won't be 100 percent perfect? Remember, progress, not perfection, is the ultimate goal.

5. **BEGINNER'S MIND:** You're not the same person you were six months ago, a year ago, or even as a child. Neither was the person you're talking to. So cut them—and you—some slack! Be flexible in your approach to baking. It's OK if you screw up a recipe. The next time you'll know how to make it better.

6. **TRUST:** Allow yourself to breathe—and relax—when you're faced with a tough situation. You have to trust the process in order for it to work out. The same goes for baking. Trust yourself to follow the instructions. Once you begin to doubt your abilities, that trust goes out the window and the baked goods go into the trash.

7. **NONSTRIVING:** This is a hard principle to grasp, especially for an overachiever like me. A lot can be resolved by not doing something—by allowing things to happen. After all, a watched pot doesn't boil. Don't force it.

8. **PATIENCE:** This is a fundamental quality of mindfulness. We cannot rush things, so slow your roll! If you take a soufflé out of the oven before it's ready, it collapses. Allow yourself to wait for something good—and when you finally get it, it will be even sweeter.

9. **GRATITUDE:** Being grateful has a positive impact on us, both mentally and physically. It's not about denying or ignoring the negative aspects of life but appreciating the good. So give thanks that you can bake! Remember, what we appreciate helps us rise.

Aunt Brenda's Pistachio Rose Water Chews

3 cups [420 g] unsalted roasted pistachios, shelled and ground

¾ cup [150 g] sugar

4 egg whites, lightly beaten

1 tsp rose water

½ tsp kosher salt

FOOD FOR THOUGHT:
As you chop the nuts, take the time to feel the knife in your hands, listen to the gentle crunching on the cutting board, and smell the sweet, nutty fragrance in the air. You are devoting your time and energy to being present for the process. The same can be said for other parts of your life too.

MAKES 24 CHEWS

To understand these meringue cookies—more like a sticky candy than a true meringue—you have to understand my Aunt Brenda. She put so much TLC into everything she baked that you could actually taste the time and energy in her sweets. These are the cookies she made for my family on holidays. You can use a food processor to pulse the pistachios into bits. If you need something to do with those leftover yolks, make my Confetti Pound Cake (page 241)!

1. Preheat the oven to 350°F [180°C] and line a baking sheet with parchment paper.

2. In a large bowl, combine the pistachios, sugar, egg whites, rose water, and salt. Stir well with a wooden spoon until the mixture sticks together and the egg whites become shiny and elastic.

3. Scoop 1 Tbsp balls of the pistachio mixture onto the prepared baking sheet, making sure to keep them at least 2 in [5 cm] apart.

4. Bake the cookies for 15 to 20 minutes, or until the edges start to brown. Allow to cool for 15 minutes, then transfer to a cooling rack to cool completely. The cookies are best eaten the same day.

Summer Fruit Crumble

1 cup [140 g] all-purpose flour

½ cup [100 g] packed
dark brown sugar

½ cup [50 g] rolled oats

½ tsp ground cinnamon

¼ tsp fine sea salt

½ cup [113 g] plus 2 Tbsp
unsalted butter

4 nectarines, peeled,
pitted, and sliced

2 ripe mangoes, peeled,
pitted, and diced

2 cups [280 g] blueberries

3 Tbsp cornstarch

½ cup [100 g] granulated sugar

2 Tbsp fresh lime juice

FOOD FOR THOUGHT:
Engage all of your senses. As
you're baking, take note of the
texture of the dough, the aroma,
the flavors. Really focus on what
you're creating.

SERVES 12

My mother's fruit crumble may be the most mindful recipe
in this book. But wait, how is a fruit crumble mindful, you
ask? The vibrant colors, the feeling of mixing the crumb
with your hands, the taste of sweetness, even the aroma of
these beautiful fruits melding together . . . the entire dessert invigorates all of your senses. Serve this bright dish
with some fresh vanilla ice cream and sink into bliss.

1. Preheat the oven to 375°F [190°C].

2. In a large bowl, combine the flour, brown sugar, oats,
    cinnamon, and salt. Cut the butter into small chunks.
    Using a pastry cutter or by hand, incorporate the butter
    into the flour mixture until clumps begin to form. Trans-
    fer the crumb mixture to a bowl, cover, and refrigerate.

3. Add the nectarines, mangoes, and blueberries to a
    9 by 13 in [23 by 33 cm] baking dish. Sprinkle the fruit
    with the cornstarch and then add the granulated
    sugar and lime juice. Mix with a wooden spoon until
    well incorporated. This will create a slurry that will
    thicken the fruit mixture as it bakes.

4. Remove the crumb mixture from the fridge and
    sprinkle it evenly over the fruit mixture.

5. Bake the crumble for about 40 minutes loosely
    covered with aluminum foil, and then uncovered for
    10 to 20 minutes, or until the crumb topping is golden
    brown and the fruit has softened. Serve warm. Store
    leftovers in the fridge for up to 3 days.

Aunt Barbara's Mandel Bread

DOUGH

1 egg

⅓ cup [65 g] sugar

½ cup [120 ml] vegetable or canola oil

1 Tbsp fresh orange juice

1 tsp vanilla extract

1½ cups [210 g] all-purpose flour

1 tsp baking powder

½ tsp fine kosher salt

½ tsp ground coriander

⅛ tsp ground nutmeg

FILLING

⅓ cup [40 g] walnuts, finely chopped

2 Tbsp mini semisweet chocolate chips

2 Tbsp sugar

1 tsp ground cinnamon

1 tsp freshly grated orange zest

MAKES 25 COOKIES (EXCELLENT FOR A LARGE PARTY)

Aunt Barbara is known for cooking for an army—a favorite is her mandel bread. I may never understand why we call it mandel bread when the final product is more like a cookie—I like to think of it as Jewish biscotti. Take a moment to really connect to your body as you prepare the dough. Let go of the pressure of perfection.

TO MAKE THE DOUGH:

1. Preheat the oven to 350°F [180°C]. Line a baking sheet with parchment paper.

2. In a large bowl, whisk together the egg, sugar, oil, orange juice, and vanilla until the mixture is well combined and uniform in color.

3. In a separate bowl, whisk together the flour, baking powder, salt, coriander, and nutmeg. Pour the dry ingredients over the wet and combine with a rubber spatula until a sticky, smooth dough forms. Transfer the dough to the prepared baking sheet and pat into an even 9 by 6 in [23 by 15 cm] rectangle, with the long side facing you.

TO MAKE THE FILLING:

1. In a medium bowl, stir together the walnuts, chocolate chips, 1 Tbsp of the sugar, ½ tsp of the cinnamon, and the orange zest.

TO ASSEMBLE AND BAKE:

1. Using a spoon, place the filling in a line down the center of the dough, going lengthwise from side to side. Use your fingers to spread the filling out, leaving about 1½ in [4 cm] of exposed dough on the top and bottom and ½ in [13 mm] on the sides. Using the parchment paper to help, fold the top and bottom dough flaps over the filling and join the edges to fully encase the filling. Pinch along all the seams, both on top and the sides, to seal the dough. Press the seams gently with your fingers to smooth them out. Combine remaining 1 Tbsp sugar and ½ tsp cinnamon and sprinkle evenly over the top of the dough.

2. Bake for 25 minutes, or until just golden brown, rotating the pan about halfway through the baking time.

3. Remove the bread from the oven and allow it to cool for 5 minutes, or until just cool enough to handle. While the bread is cooling, lower the oven temperature to 250°F [120°C].

4. Using a sharp knife, cut the bread crosswise into ½ in [13 mm] sections and place them cut-side up on the baking sheet. Place the baking sheet back into the oven and bake for about 45 minutes. This will allow the bread to dry out and give this treat its signature crisp texture.

5. Serve immediately while warm, or let cool to room temperature. If you want to save some (as the recipe makes quite a few), store them in a breathable container such as a paper bag or wicker basket so that they stay crispy for up to 5 days.

BAKING AFFIRMATION:
Today I am letting things turn out the way they turn out.

The Not-So-Rough Puff Pear Pastry

ROUGH PUFF

2 cups [280 g] all-purpose flour

1 tsp table salt

1¼ cups [275 g] cold unsalted butter, thinly sliced

½ cup [120 ml] ice-cold water

FILLING

2 red pears, cored and thinly sliced

1 tsp fresh lemon juice

2 sprigs of rosemary, torn into rough small pieces

1 egg

¼ cup [85 g] honey

NOTE: *Using store-bought puff pastry dough works well too, if you need to put one less thing on your mind.*

SERVES 8

My Great-Grandma Adina from Guatemala was the number one baking champion—the baker of all bakers, if you will. Every fall, she would pick apples from my grandmother's garden in New Jersey and make us homemade puff pastry filled with fresh pears and apples. This recipe is an homage to that memory. A lot of people read "puff pastry" and run for the hills, but this version is so easy that you don't have to! While you roll and roll and roll this dough, let go of the fear and give in to the puff.

TO MAKE THE ROUGH PUFF:

1. In a large bowl, whisk together the flour and salt. Toss the butter in the flour mixture to coat it and then add the water. Use a rubber spatula to work everything into a dough, then form the dough into a rough, flat rectangle. Wrap the dough in plastic wrap and refrigerate it for at least 1 hour and up to 24 hours.

2. After the dough has chilled, flour your work surface and a rolling pin and roll the dough into a rectangle about ½ in [13 mm] thick. It will be cracked and rough—and that is just fine! Fold the dough into thirds in the shape of a letter, rotate the dough 90 degrees, and reroll it to about ½ in [13 mm] thick. Continue this process two more times, or until the dough begins to soften. As soon as the dough begins to soften, fold it into thirds and rewrap it in plastic

cont.

wrap. Refrigerate for at least 2 hours, or up to overnight.

3. Remove the dough from the fridge and repeat the rolling and folding process twice more. Then, roll the dough out to ¼ in [6 mm] thickness. Use a large knife or pizza cutter to cut the dough in half lengthwise, then three times widthwise into eight equal rectangles.

TO MAKE THE FILLING AND BAKE:

1. Preheat the oven to 425°F [220°C]. Line a baking sheet with parchment paper.

2. In a bowl, toss the pear slices with the lemon juice. Layer a couple of pear slices crosswise on each section of pastry, sprinkle them evenly with rosemary, then slightly pull over edges of pastry (about ½ in [13 mm]), leaving the filling mostly exposed.

3. In a small bowl, whisk the egg and 1 tsp of water. Brush the egg wash along the edges of the pastry. Drizzle the honey over the filled pastries.

4. Place the pastries on the prepared baking sheet and bake for 25 minutes, or until puffy and flaky. Remove from the oven and serve the pastries immediately or let cool to room temperature.

BAKING AFFIRMATION:
Today I will trust the process and let go of preconceptions.

Marbled Rye Breadsticks

LIGHT RYE

½ cup [120 ml] warm water, about 110°F [45°C]

1 tsp sugar

½ tsp active dry yeast

1 cup [140 g] bread flour

½ cup [55 g] light rye flour

½ tsp table salt

½ tsp whole caraway seeds

1 Tbsp olive oil

1½ tsp light molasses

DARK RYE

½ cup [120 ml] warm water, about 110°F [45°C]

1 tsp sugar

½ tsp active dry yeast

1 cup [140 g] bread flour

½ cup [55 g] light rye flour

1 Tbsp unsweetened cocoa powder

½ tsp table salt

½ tsp whole caraway seeds

1 Tbsp olive oil

1½ tsp light molasses

cont.

MAKES 24

My friend Michael always jokes, "I'm pretty sure that if you looked at my blood under a microscope, you'd find rye floating around in there somewhere." These thin breadsticks show off a beautiful twist pattern that grabs your attention immediately. The caraway seeds add a bright, punchy kick that will keep you and your guests coming back for more. I recommend serving these with lots and lots of warmed butter.

TO MAKE THE LIGHT RYE:

1. In a small bowl, combine the warm water, sugar, and yeast. Set aside for 10 minutes while the yeast activates.

2. Meanwhile, in a large bowl, whisk together the flours, salt, and caraway seeds. Make a well in the center of the mixture and add the olive oil, molasses, and yeast mixture. Use a wooden spoon to mix the ingredients until the dough becomes combined enough to begin kneading with your hands.

3. At this point, you can either continue to knead the dough in the bowl or turn the dough out onto a lightly oiled work surface. Knead the dough for 5 to 7 minutes, or until it becomes smooth. It should be tacky at this point.

4. Lightly oil a large bowl, form the dough into a ball, and place the dough in the oiled bowl. Roll it around to coat it in the oil, then cover the bowl with a damp kitchen towel. Set aside to rise for 1½ hours.

cont.

EGG WASH

1 egg

1 tsp water

Kosher salt, for sprinkling

TO MAKE THE DARK RYE:

1. In a small bowl, combine the warm water, sugar, and yeast. Set aside for 10 minutes while the yeast activates.

2. Meanwhile, in a large bowl, whisk together the flours, cocoa powder, salt, and caraway seeds. Make a well in the center of the mixture and add the olive oil, molasses, and yeast mixture. Use a wooden spoon to mix the ingredients until the dough becomes combined enough to begin kneading with your hands.

3. At this point, you can either continue to knead the dough in the bowl or turn the dough out onto a lightly oiled work surface. Knead the dough for 5 to 7 minutes, or until it becomes smooth. It should be tacky at this point.

4. Lightly oil a large bowl, form the dough into a ball, and place the dough in the oiled bowl. Roll it around to coat it in the oil, then cover the bowl with a damp kitchen towel. Set aside to rise for 1½ hours.

TO ASSEMBLE:

1. Line two baking sheets with parchment paper.

2. Once the doughs have risen, cut each ball in half. Lightly oil your work surface again and use your hands to pat half of each dough into a square about ¼ in [6 mm] thick. Cover the remaining dough halves with a damp kitchen towel while you work.

cont.

3. Use a large kitchen knife to slice the doughs into thin strips, each about ½ in [13 mm] wide. Take one strip of light dough and one strip of dark dough, pinch the tops together, and twist them together. Pinch the dough together at the bottom. Set aside on the prepared baking sheet. Repeat with the remaining dough.

4. Cover the braided breadsticks with damp kitchen towels and allow to rise for another 30 minutes. Then, roll each breadstick on your work surface with both of your hands until the dough forms a long, thin breadstick with a swirl pattern running throughout.

TO MAKE THE EGG WASH AND BAKE:

1. Preheat the oven to 350°F [180°C].

2. In a small bowl, whisk the egg and water together. Use a pastry brush to apply it to the tops of the breadsticks. Sprinkle them with salt.

3. Arrange the breadsticks about 1 in [2.5 cm] apart on the prepared baking sheets and bake for 10 minutes. The breadsticks will be soft and spongy to the touch.

4. Remove from the oven and let cool for 5 minutes. Serve warm. Store leftovers in the fridge in an air-tight container for up to 4 days.

FOOD FOR THOUGHT:
While you knead your dough, do a body scan check-in. What do you feel at your fingertips? How do your arms feel?

Lime Chiffon Cake

WITH HONEY-ROASTED PISTACHIOS AND ORANGE BLOSSOM WHIPPED CREAM

CAKE

2 cups [280 g] all-purpose flour

1½ cups [300 g] sugar

1 tsp table salt

½ tsp baking powder

½ tsp ground cardamom

6 eggs, separated, at room temperature

¾ cup [180 ml] fresh lime juice

Grated zest of 2 limes, plus more for topping

½ cup [120 ml] canola oil

½ tsp vanilla extract

½ tsp cream of tartar

TOPPING

Homemade Whipped Cream (page 39), mixed with ⅛ tsp orange blossom water

Honey-Roasted Pistachios (recipe follows)

SERVES 8 TO 12

This cake is all about lightness. While the baking process is a little involved, think of it as an opportunity to meditate on the lightness within yourself—or how to lift up what's weighing you down. Its bright lime flavor pairs with the airy texture of chiffon cake. The fluffy layers of orange blossom whipped cream bring a scrumptious, floral aspect to your palate, while ground cardamom adds just enough earthiness to keep you grounded.

TO MAKE THE CAKE:

1. Preheat the oven to 350°F [180°C].

2. Grease two 9 in [23 cm] round cake pans with 2 Tbsp of coconut oil and sprinkle evenly with 2 Tbsp of flour, shaking off any excess.

3. In a large bowl, whisk together the flour, sugar, salt, baking powder, and cardamom. Set aside.

4. In a medium bowl, whisk together the egg yolks, lime juice, lime zest, canola oil, and vanilla. Add the wet ingredients to the dry ingredients and whisk until a thick, well-combined batter forms. Set aside.

5. In the bowl of a stand mixer fitted with the whisk attachment, or in a medium bowl using a handheld electric mixer, beat the egg whites and cream of tartar on high speed until stiff peaks form, about 8 minutes. The time can vary, depending on the mixer; just be sure not to over- or under-whip.

cont.

baking and will fall if jostled too much. If you have little ones who like to stomp around the house (what little ones don't, right?), then maybe save this cake for nap time or when the kids are playing outside.

FOOD FOR THOUGHT:
This cake requires whisking and beating, patience, and a gentle hand. When you can be mindful of your actions, you can develop a type of self-control that will take you to beautiful places!

6.   Here comes the most important part: This step is what makes a true chiffon cake. Using a rubber spatula, very lightly scrape half of the egg white mixture into the egg yolk batter. Begin folding the two mixtures together with broad, slow, circular motions until the thick batter begins to fluff up. Add the rest of the egg white mixture and continue folding everything together until just combined. If you overmix the batter, or mix it too aggressively, the cake won't have its signature airiness.

7.   Very gently divide the batter between the prepared cake pans. Bake for 20 to 25 minutes, or until the cakes are golden brown (see Note). Remove the cakes from the oven and allow to cool completely before removing them from the pans.

8.   Once the cakes are cooled, using a serrated knife, cut the tops off to create a level surface.

TO ASSEMBLE THE CAKE:

1.   Use a spatula to spread the whipped cream over the first cake in a 1 in [2.5 cm] layer. At this point, depending on how much you love pistachios, you can either sprinkle some over the whipped cream or go ahead and add the next cake layer. Repeat spreading the whipped cream over the top layer and then top with the pistachios and extra lime zest in whatever decorative pattern feels best.

2.   You can serve immediately or refrigerate this cake and serve it cold. It's excellent with a hot cup of tea. Store leftovers in the fridge for up to 3 days.

cont.

Honey-Roasted Pistachios

MAKES 1 CUP

1 cup [140 g] shelled, unsalted pistachios, raw or roasted

2 Tbsp honey

Pinch of salt

You know what's great? Pistachios. They're a staple of Syrian desserts, and you should always have some honey-roasted pistachios on hand. Nuts are healthy, so why wouldn't honey-roasted nuts be healthy too? I'll pretend if you will. Store them in an airtight container for up to 1 week, if they make it that long. However, if you eat them all right off the baking sheet, you won't have to share.

1. Preheat the oven to 400°F [200°C] and line a baking sheet with parchment paper.

2. In a small bowl, mix together the pistachios, honey, and salt. Spread the mixture evenly on the prepared baking sheet and roast for 5 to 7 minutes, or until the honey begins to caramelize.

3. Remove the pistachios from the oven and let cool. Use in your favorite desserts or snack on them straight from the pan. Store in an airtight container at room temperature for up to 1 week.

NOTE: *You can use salted pistachios if unsalted aren't available. Just be sure to eliminate the salt from the recipe.*

Grandma Raquel's Dark Chocolate Mousse

4 oz [115 g] dark baking chocolate, about 70% cacao

1 Tbsp unsalted butter

1 Tbsp Kahlúa

½ cup [120 ml] heavy cream

3 Tbsp powdered sugar

½ tsp vanilla extract

3 eggs, separated

½ tsp cream of tartar

SERVES 8

Grandma Raquel's mousse was always a family favorite, maybe because she made it extra boozy. She always said it was an excuse to drink! While the alcohol in this version is toned down, feel free to kick it up a notch to suit your taste buds. This recipe is easy, fun, and delicious, and you need only a few bites to satisfy your sweet tooth. Feel free to top it with Homemade Whipped Cream (page 39).

1. In a microwave-safe bowl, combine the chocolate and butter. Microwave in 20-second intervals, stirring well in between, until the chocolate is completely melted. Add the Kahlúa. Stir to incorporate the ingredients fully and set aside.

2. In the bowl of a stand mixer fitted with the paddle attachment, or in a medium bowl using a handheld electric mixer, beat the heavy cream, powdered sugar, and vanilla until stiff peaks form. Start mixing on low speed, then increase to medium, and then to high. This will take several minutes. Once you have stiff peaks, immediately place the whipped cream in the fridge to chill until needed.

3. In the clean bowl of a stand mixer fitted with the whisk attachment, or in a medium bowl using a handheld electric mixer, beat the egg whites and cream of tartar until thick, firm peaks form. Start mixing on low speed, then increase to medium, and then to high. Set the whipped egg whites aside.

cont.

4. In a large bowl, combine the cooled, but still liquid, chocolate and the egg yolks and use a rubber spatula to gently fold them together. The mixture will not be fully combined at this point. Add the whipped cream to the chocolate mixture and gently fold together until mostly combined. Your goal is to keep the mixture as airy as possible, so be sure not to overwork it.

5. Add half of the whipped egg whites to the chocolate mixture and use your spatula to fold them together until almost completely combined. Then, add the remaining egg whites. Use your rubber spatula to scrape down the sides of your bowl and fold the mousse mixture together until it is smooth and well incorporated. Again, your goal is to combine the mixture with as few folds as possible to keep everything light and airy.

6. Either gently scoop the mixture into separate small serving dishes or into one larger dish. Place the mousse in the fridge for at least 2 hours to set. Store leftovers in the fridge for up to 3 days.

BAKING AFFIRMATION:
When I check into the kitchen, I check out of the outside world.

Lemon Ginger Bundt Cake

CAKE

3 cups [420 g] all-purpose flour

¼ cup [40 g] finely diced crystallized ginger

3 Tbsp grated lemon zest

1 tsp baking soda

1 tsp fine sea salt

1 cup [220 g] unsalted butter, at room temperature

2⅓ cups [465 g] granulated sugar

6 eggs

⅓ cup [80 ml] fresh lemon juice

1 cup [240 g] sour cream (low fat is OK, nonfat is not)

GLAZE

⅔ cup [80 g] powdered sugar

2 Tbsp unsalted butter, melted

1 Tbsp fresh lemon juice

½ tsp ground ginger

SERVES 8

Taking a deep breath is a great way to practice mindfulness. Pairing deep breathing with gorgeous aromas like the ginger and lemon in this cake can really invigorate the senses. I like to think of these as baking essential oils, helping to facilitate meditation while in the kitchen. And Bundt cakes are always great for sharing, so go share your newfound peace by having a bite with friends.

TO MAKE THE CAKE:

1. Preheat the oven to 350°F [180°C]. Butter and flour or use nonstick cooking spray to coat a standard 12 cup [2.8 L] Bundt pan (or two smaller 6 cup [1.4 L] Bundt pans).

2. In a large bowl, whisk together the flour, ginger, lemon zest, baking soda, and salt. Make sure all the tiny chunks of ginger are covered in a layer of flour so they don't sink to the bottom of the cake. Set aside.

3. In the bowl of a stand mixer fitted with the paddle attachment, or in a medium bowl using an electric hand mixer, cream the butter and granulated sugar for 3 to 4 minutes, until light and fluffy. Scrape down the sides of the bowl as needed. (It's always needed.)

4. Add the eggs, one at a time, beating well after each addition. Add the lemon juice and beat to combine.

cont.

5. Turn the mixer to low speed and alternate adding the flour mixture, then the sour cream, until the mixture is combined. Do not overmix here. Pour the batter into the prepared Bundt pan(s) (I use a large cookie scoop for this). Smooth the top of the batter with an offset spatula.

6. Bake the full Bundt cake for 55 to 60 minutes or the half-size Bundt cakes for 30 minutes, or until the cake is golden brown, tests cleanly with a cake tester, and pulls away from the sides of the pan. Let cool in the pan on a cooling rack for at least 20 minutes, and then turn out carefully onto a rack to cool completely.

TO MAKE THE GLAZE:

1. While the cake is cooling, in a small bowl, whisk together the powdered sugar, melted butter, lemon juice, and ground ginger. If it is too thick, add another few drops of lemon juice. If it is too stiff, add another 1 to 2 tsp of powdered sugar. Pour the glaze over the cooled cake(s) and let set for at least an hour.

TO SERVE:

1. Serve immediately or store tightly wrapped in plastic wrap at room temperature for 2 to 3 days. The unglazed cake can be kept in the freezer for 30 days.

FOOD FOR THOUGHT:
Allow the aromatherapy aspects of this cake to calm and sharpen your senses all at once. Breathe deeply and with intention.

Baked Pumpkin Donuts to Fall For WITH VANILLA GLAZE

DONUTS

1¾ cups [210 g] cake flour

1½ tsp baking powder

1 tsp ground cinnamon

½ tsp fine sea salt

½ tsp ground cardamom

¼ tsp ground ginger

⅛ tsp ground allspice

Pinch of nutmeg

Pinch of freshly ground black pepper

1½ cups [400 g] canned
pumpkin purée

1½ cups [300 g] packed
light brown sugar

½ cup [120 ml] olive oil

3 eggs

GLAZE

1½ cups [180 g] powdered sugar

2 Tbsp olive oil

2 Tbsp maple syrup

1 to 2 Tbsp hot water

Pumpkin seeds (pepitas),
for topping

MAKES 24 DONUTS

Pumpkin reminds everyone of fall. While some of us adore the chilly change of seasons, many people are affected by seasonal depression. If you are one of those people, or just someone who happens to be feeling down on a cool, brisk day, I encourage you to give this recipe a try. The fragrant spices and warmth of a fresh donut give you something to look forward to in a time where that feeling can be difficult to find.

TO MAKE THE DONUTS:

1. Preheat the oven to 350°F [180°C] and spray a donut pan (or two if you have them) with nonstick cooking spray.

2. In a medium bowl, whisk the flour, baking powder, cinnamon, sea salt, cardamom, ginger, allspice, and nutmeg.

3. In the bowl of a stand mixer fitted with the paddle attachment, or in a medium bowl using a handheld electric mixer, beat the pumpkin purée and light brown sugar together for 1 minute. With the mixer running at low-medium speed, slowly drizzle in the olive oil, then add the eggs one at a time, beating after each addition until the batter is smooth. Add the dry ingredients and mix until incorporated.

4. Using a small cookie scoop (or a large zip-top bag with the tip of one corner snipped off), add about 3 Tbsp of batter to each well of the donut pan. Bake

cont.

for 15 minutes, or until the donuts are golden and spring back when lightly touched with your finger.

TO MAKE THE GLAZE:

1. When you remove the donuts from the oven, in a small bowl, combine the powdered sugar, olive oil, maple syrup, and water and stir until smooth. The glaze will be opaque; if you want a thinner glaze, add extra water, 1 Tbsp at a time, until it is the desired consistency.

2. Let the donuts cool on a cooling rack for 3 minutes, then flip out onto a rack set over a baking sheet. Dunk the top of the donut in the glaze twice, then let the extra drip back into the bowl. Sprinkle on pumpkin seeds while the glaze is wet and sticky. Let cool on the cooling rack until the glaze hardens to a glossy shine. These are best eaten right away.

BAKING AFFIRMATION:
I will allow things to happen in their own time.

Chai-Soaked Pear Shortbread Bars

BARS

1 cup [140 g] all-purpose flour

¼ cup [50 g] granulated sugar

1 tsp ground chai tea (from about 1 tea bag)

¼ tsp baking powder

¼ tsp ground ginger

¼ tsp ground allspice

Pinch of ground cloves

Pinch of kosher salt

½ cup [110 g] cold, unsalted butter, cut into ½ in [13 mm] pieces

TOPPING

5 ripe pears

2 tsp ground chai tea (from about 2 teabags)

1 tsp cornstarch

½ tsp ground ginger

1 Tbsp apple cider vinegar

MAKES 16 BARS

Listen, my three o'clock chai saves my life every single workday. When I'm fading and hear my bed calling my name, I brew a cup of tea, close my eyes, and hold the mug just under my nose. I take a minute to feel the warmth of the tea in my hands. The scent of the spices works through my body and into my mind, letting me come to a quiet and present place. It resets me and reminds me that the small moments in life are worth showing up for. These bars are baked with that same feeling—and you don't have to wait for that afternoon slump to have one! So whenever you need a little pick-me-up or a quiet snack break, have one (or two).

1. Preheat the oven to 350°F [180°C]. Lightly oil an 8 in [20 cm] square pan.

2. In a large bowl, whisk together the flour, sugar, and tea. Add the baking powder, ginger, allspice, cloves, and salt, and toss to combine. Add the pieces of cold butter and toss to coat in the flour mixture. Use your fingertips to smash the butter into the flour mixture, working until no large pieces remain and you have lots of moist crumbs that hold together easily when squeezed.

3. Scatter the dough evenly across the bottom of the prepared pan and flatten into an even layer, working it into the corners and against the sides. Bake the shortbread until lightly golden across the surface, 25 to 30 minutes. Remove the pan from the oven and lower the temperature to 300°F [150°C].

TO MAKE THE TOPPING:

1. Core and cut pears into 1 in [2.5 cm] chunks and put them in a large bowl. They don't have to be perfect—a mix of sizes adds texture.

2. In a small bowl, mix the tea, cornstarch, and ginger. Add the tea mixture and the apple cider vinegar to the sliced pears and toss to coat.

TO BAKE:

1. Spread the pears on the shortbread and cover it evenly. Bake for 25 to 30 minutes, or until the topping is light golden brown and firm to the touch.

2. Remove from the oven and let the bars cool completely in the pan. For a cleaner cut, transfer the cooled pan to the fridge and chill until the bottom of the pan is cold to the touch, about 1 hour. Slice into sixteen squares. Store leftovers in the fridge for up to 2 days.

FOOD FOR THOUGHT:
A cluttered kitchen makes for a cluttered mind. If you can keep your kitchen organized, you'll minimize distractions and feel more comfortable when you set out to bake.

Heaven and Hell Cake

CAKE

2 cups [280 g] all-purpose flour

1½ tsp baking soda

¾ tsp baking powder

¾ tsp fine sea salt

¾ cup [165 g] unsalted butter,
at room temperature

2 cups [400 g] plus 2 Tbsp
granulated sugar

¾ cup [60 g] unsweetened
cocoa powder

2 tsp vanilla extract

3 eggs, at room temperature

¼ cup [60 ml] whole milk

FROSTING

1 cup [220 g] unsalted butter,
at room temperature

One 14 oz [400 g] jar
marshmallow creme

2 tsp vanilla extract (use
clear if you want to keep
the frosting pure white)

Pinch of fine sea salt

2 cups [240 g] powdered sugar

Cocoa powder, for topping

SERVES 10

There's a devil and an angel in each of us, right? Maybe even more devil than we like to admit. (Insert evil smirk.) This cake allows you to be a little of both. The cake is sinfully delicious while the frosting is perfectly sweet (and maybe a little innocent too). As you bake, embrace all sides of yourself. Imagine how boring you would be if you were only an angel! All the messy stuff is part of you. Combining every aspect of yourself creates a fascinating human experience.

TO MAKE THE CAKE:

1. Preheat the oven to 350°F [180°C]. Butter two 9 in [23 cm] round cake pans or spray with nonstick cooking spray and line the bottoms with a circle of parchment paper.

2. In a large bowl, combine the flour, baking soda, baking powder, and salt. Set aside.

3. In the bowl of a stand mixer fitted with the paddle attachment, or in a medium bowl using a handheld electric mixer, beat the butter until smooth. Slowly add the granulated sugar and beat until combined, about 3 minutes. Turn off the mixer, scrape down the sides, and add the cocoa powder and vanilla. Add the eggs one at a time, mixing after each addition.

4. In a small saucepan over medium-high heat, combine 1¼ cups [300 ml] water and milk and heat until almost boiling. Watch carefully, as it can boil over very quickly. Remove from the heat.

cont.

5. Add the dry ingredients to the butter mixture a little bit at a time, stirring and scraping the sides after each addition. Carefully add the milk mixture. Scrape down the sides of the bowl and mix again until smooth. The batter will be much wetter than a usual cake batter. Divide equally between the two prepared pans.

6. Bake for 30 to 35 minutes, until the center springs back when touched.

7. Let cool for 15 minutes, flip out onto a cooling rack, and cool completely before frosting. (You can wrap and freeze the unfrosted cake layers for up to 2 months.)

TO FROST AND SERVE:

1. While the cake is cooling, in the bowl of a stand mixer fitted with the paddle attachment or using a handheld electric mixer, beat the butter, marshmallow creme, vanilla, and salt on medium-low speed until smooth. Add the powdered sugar, a little at a time, and mix until combined. Use immediately.

2. Place one cake layer on a cake stand or plate. (Cut off any domed tops with a serrated knife so it frosts evenly.) Spread about one-third of the frosting to the edges with an offset spatula. Top with the other cake (cut-side down) and use the rest of the frosting to frost the top and sides of the cake. Sprinkle the cocoa powder on top.

3. Store leftovers in the fridge for up to 3 days.

FOOD FOR THOUGHT:
Accept yourself as you are.
Perfection is boring.

Choose-Your-Own Scone

BASE SCONE

½ cup plus 2 Tbsp [150 ml] buttermilk

1 egg

2 cups [280 g] all-purpose flour

⅓ cup [65 g] sugar

1 Tbsp baking powder

1 tsp fine sea salt

½ tsp baking soda

½ cup [110 g] cold, unsalted butter, cut into small chunks

NOTE: *Scones can be cut in a variety of shapes (wedges, round, or square). Once cut, unbaked scones can be stored in an airtight container in the freezer for up to 1 month. Place frozen scone dough on a lined baking sheet and add 2 minutes to the baking time. Once baked, they are best eaten the same day.*

MAKES 8 SCONES

Commitment is scary. This cute little recipe allows you to combat that fear by encouraging you to choose your own adventure. Feeling sweet? Savory? I've got you covered. And it's OK if your mood changes! Be mindful of where your inner voice wants to lead you today with these low-pressure scones.

TO MAKE THE BASE SCONE:

1. In a small bowl, whisk together the buttermilk and egg. Set aside.

2. In a large bowl, combine the flour, sugar, baking powder, salt, and baking soda. Add the butter into the flour mixture and mix the butter into the dry ingredients with your fingers until you get small chunks of butter that are covered with flour. Place the flour and butter mixture in the freezer for 5 minutes to re-chill. Remove from the freezer. If making blueberry or savory Cheddar and chive scones, add the mix-ins and toss carefully to coat in the flour. Add the buttermilk mixture slowly and gently mix with a rubber spatula until combined.

3. Turn the dough out onto a well-floured work surface. Roll out the dough into a rectangle that is about ¾ in [2 cm] thick. Fold the dough into thirds in the shape of a letter, cut the now smaller rectangle crosswise into four equal pieces, and cut each piece into two triangles.

cont.

4. Put the scone wedges on a baking sheet lined with parchment paper. Chill for at least 1 hour in the fridge.

5. Preheat the oven to 400°F [200°C].

6. Bake the scones for 16 to 20 minutes, or until puffy and golden brown. Cool on the baking sheet for 10 minutes, then transfer to a wire cooling rack and cool completely. If you made sweet scones and want to add a glaze, do it now. Store leftovers in the fridge for up to 2 days.

OPTIONAL FLAVOR COMBOS

LEMON BLUEBERRY

Add the grated zest of 1 lemon to the dry ingredients and fold ⅓ cup [45 g] of blueberries into the chilled flour and butter mixture before stirring in the wet ingredients. Glaze with ½ cup [60 g] of powdered sugar mixed with 2 Tbsp of buttermilk.

MAPLE WALNUT

Add 1 tsp of ground cinnamon and ⅓ cup [40 g] of toasted and chopped walnuts to the dry ingredients. Glaze with ½ cup [60 g] of powdered sugar mixed with 3 Tbsp of maple syrup.

SAVORY CHEDDAR AND CHIVE

Cut the sugar back to 2 Tbsp and add ½ cup [40 g] of shredded Cheddar cheese and ¼ cup [5 g] of chopped chives to the chilled flour and butter mixture before stirring in the wet ingredients.

BAKING AFFIRMATION:
I can accept and understand everyone has their own personal preferences—and favorite flavor combinations.

Finding

Comfort

Let's take a moment to talk about grief and loss. First, they never seem to happen at the right time. In fact, is there ever a right time? (Unfortunately, no.) But the one thing I've learned throughout my life, and as a therapist, is that no matter how impactful a loss is—and the pain that comes with it—we're able to find ways to comfort ourselves (and others) during these times.

In Judaism, we don't wait to bury those who have passed. In fact, it's usually no more than twenty-four hours later. The key here is to start the mourning process quickly because acceptance (the final stage of the grieving process) is healing. This grieving period is called shiva—Hebrew for "seven"—and lasts for a full week. There are a few traditions associated with this process, but none is more essential than the tradition around food.

Years ago, I lost my Grandma Peggy. Yes, that grandma whom I baked with and inspired me with her Syrian culinary expertise and flavors. I learned my way around the kitchen from her. So my family sat shiva. During that time, our goal was to focus on the loss and relive our memories of her (in fact, when someone does pass, we usually say "May their memory be a blessing"). Sitting shiva forces us to confront our grief. The last thing on our minds is "What are we going to eat?" That's why guests who come to pay their respects always bring food, because food is the ultimate comfort! (And don't show up with flowers; that's a goy thing.)

The grieving process is not just limited to the loss of a loved one. It can be for a divorce, or breakup, or friendship that's run its course. Or we can even grieve the way things were, like the carefree you from your childhood. The question is, how do we go about finding comfort when faced with difficult, life-altering situations?

If you're anything like me, I tend to jump headfirst into making—and then eating—my favorite comfort food. This was especially true after one of my closest childhood friends, Leon Antar, passed away tragically. (May his memory be a blessing.) I was comforted knowing I can still create and not just stuff my face. Maybe you watch your favorite movie or listen to a particular song. These are all ways to find comfort. Some people, like my Great-Aunt Frida, find comfort while also giving comfort to others. After her teenage daughter—my cousin—passed away, my great-aunt started a foundation to keep her memory alive by inspiring and providing aid to those who needed it.

Our memories are tied to experiences, smells, and flavors, so it's no wonder that baking can be so comforting. When we bake, we're not just connecting to the memory of that experience or the person with whom we shared that food. Baking connects us back to our family history, religion, or culture—it's a story of where we've come from, even when the narrator has passed. For example, when I make Grandma Peggy's Kanafeh (page 112), I'm connected to my grandfather's story: the town where he grew up, his emigration from Syria to America, and the traditional flavors of Aleppo (they use rose water instead of vanilla as their favorite extract). Rose water is Syrian baking's holy water; it's a specialty of Syrian desserts and one that's so potent it skyrockets me back to the old land. I know that I may never be able to get back to Syria, but I still find comfort in making the dish and what it represents.

Baking forces us to face our feelings. It's like sitting shiva. While you might be numb from pain, the rote actions of assembling a dish require you to be "present" in a different way than mindfulness or self-care. Your hands keep your body physically alert, giving your mind the ability to pay attention to what you're feeling. They're the vessels for letting your emotions out. And it's totally OK if you cry as you work through a recipe. Crying is healing! (Just be sure to not get any tears in that batter, though.)

Simply put, baking is a comforting experience from start to finish. Whipping cream is very soothing. Kneading dough—a very versatile medium for Baking Therapy—absorbs our emotional energy really well. The piping skills used when decorating a cake can mimic what Grandma used to do; it's a great way to honor her (or anyone else who used to bake with and for you). And then we have the aromas, which fill our hearts and warm us from the inside. Trust me when I say that nothing smells as delicious as freshly baked Challah Caramel Bread Pudding (page 123).

Finally, getting to eat what you baked is even more comforting. Why else would we call it comfort food? It has the power to comfort not only ourselves, but others as well. One of my favorite lines from the Marvel Cinematic Universe is "What is grief if not love persevering?" (How beautiful is that?!) And the best way to keep love going? A little baked goodness that comes from the heart, either for yourself or for others who are going through their own difficult situations.

Just remember that healing is a process, whether it's seeking closure or easing the emotional toll of a loss. We can't rush it, like we can't rush through a recipe; a rushed recipe never bakes properly. And you can't ignore what you're feeling either. If you stuff—or hide—the feelings away, they can eventually consume you. "You gotta feel to heal" is something I tell my patients.

That pint of Breyer's Light isn't going to bring things back to the way they were. And neither will baking a tray of decadent, soft, and fudgy brownies (although they do taste damn good). Baking, and eating, aren't magical fixes that send grief and loss away. But they help ease the burden and help ease us into a place of acceptance. They teach us three things in the process: create, enjoy, and let go. We create something new from the ingredients and learn to appreciate what each brings to the recipe. We enjoy what we've baked once it's out of the oven. We let go by acknowledging how that treat made us feel, what the empty plate once held, and that the event is over.

We all know the adage "When life hands you lemons, make lemonade." Don't get me wrong: I love a good lemonade. But it can be too tart sometimes. The next time life hands you a lemon—or three—bake them into a delicious tart. Or use them as a garnish on top. Baking goes a long way, and you can take comfort in that.

Quick Session

BAKING THROUGH THE FIVE STAGES OF GRIEF

The first session with a patient experiencing grief is usually very intense; they tend to relive the trauma. As a therapist, I need to tread carefully and understand who all the people in the story are, what their connection to my patient is, and who my patient is all at once. So you can only imagine the magnitude of my first grief session that happened to be one of my very first sessions as a therapist.

A patient had experienced the unimaginable—losing several loved ones in a short amount of time. Each of these losses elicited grief and compounded the trauma he was going through. What made his grief more complicated was the strained relationships he had with them. At first, he was closed off, unwilling to explore the deep-seated nature of his relationships. It's our mind's way of trying to make sense of everything to lessen the burden of truth. A little fail-safe, if you will. But I felt the one thing that could help him not only open up but also start to heal: baking.

So, we stepped into the kitchen for his sessions: It was a great way to get him to start to open up and also create some comfort food along the way. The process helped untangle the web of emotions he was experiencing through the five stages of grief.

DENIAL: In the first stage of grief, you don't accept what has happened. Truth be told, you're kind of in a numb emotional state. But baking helps "zap" you out of it. From the aromatherapy to the movements, your senses and body are woken up to bring you out of the fog and into what's happening in the kitchen.

ANGER: You're mad at whoever has left you. You may even curse them out. You recall that last conversation, whether it was good or bad. Baking is a safe way to release that anger (if you're stuck in your anger phase, check out the Letting Go of Frustration chapter, page 166). To work through anger, channel that energy from your head into your hands and into the batter or dough; you'll be transforming it into something beautiful and delicious.

BARGAINING: This is our brain saying, "What if" or "If only." You're willing to do anything to have them back. "Please send them back to me and I promise I'll do X." Baking brings a stillness to this phase of grief. You're removing yourself from the noise and focusing on yourself. There's nothing else you can do—especially while you bake—that will help bring you that much closer to acceptance.

DEPRESSION: This is when we really start to feel the loss of a loved one. The bargaining has failed, and reality has set in. As the sadness grows, we tend to turn inward and isolate. But baking makes it easier to emerge. Take a recipe one step at time. It's not asking you to take giant actions; your mind (and soul) are not ready for that. Whatever you're capable of doing, do it. Take your time to work through your feelings—and that recipe.

ACCEPTANCE: This is the final step of grief. The pain of the loss is still there, but we accept the reality of what has happened—we're not resisting that reality. As we bake, we have to accept the results when the oven timer goes off. If the cake is lopsided or the cookies are not perfect, that's OK! We learn to let go in that moment, and that cathartic release is one we often search for when processing grief.

My patient loved apple pie; it reminded him of simpler times growing up with his family. Before all the trauma. Before the scars formed. But the process of baking together allowed him to open up to me and to himself. While he may never get what he needed from his family, he understood he was capable of love and being loved. Honestly, it took more than a few sessions to get there, but in the end, baking gave him a gift: the ability to envision a future filled with hope.

Jack's Famous Challah

2⅓ cups [560 ml] warm water, about 110°F [45°C]

½ cup [100 g] sugar, plus a pinch for the egg wash

2 Tbsp active dry yeast

9 cups [1.26 kg] bread flour

2 Tbsp kosher salt, plus a pinch for the egg wash

½ cup [120 ml] canola oil or ½ cup [110 g] margarine, melted

2 eggs

1 tsp vanilla extract (optional)

2 Tbsp honey

2 egg yolks

3 Tbsp za'atar (optional)

MAKES 3 LOAVES

This is it. This is the reason you're reading this book: my Madonna-approved challah. But it's really my family's perfected recipe that I baked with Grandma Peggy. I'm just baking it for a new generation through my company, JackBakes. Grandma Peggy taught me so much about life, family, and myself every Thursday afternoon. This was the one after-school activity where I felt truly comfortable being myself—the kitchen and my grandmother didn't judge me. This challah not only saved my life when I was younger, but it has also gotten me through some very difficult situations: being fired from my family's business, supporting myself through grad school, and even helping me connect with others at the Kabbalah Centre the first time I didn't do Shabbat with my family. (It was there that Madonna tried—and gushed about—my challah.)

But what I really love about this challah is the process for making it. Kneading the dough, letting it rise, and braiding each strand takes time, energy, and love. The final result is a luscious, thick, and—dare I say it?—sexy loaf of bread. Challah-lujah! Note: I love challah, but if this is too much for you to make, feel free to cut the quantities in half! You'll make two smaller loaves, but make sure to bake them for only 25 to 30 minutes.

1. In a medium bowl, combine 1 cup [240 ml] of the warm water, the sugar, and yeast. Set aside for 10 minutes while the yeast activates.

cont.

2. In the bowl of a stand mixer fitted with the dough hook attachment, or in a medium bowl using a handheld electric mixer, add the flour, make a well in the center, and bury the salt in the well. Add the canola oil, eggs, honey, vanilla (if using), remaining 1⅓ cups [320 ml] of warm water, and the yeast mixture, making sure no sediment is left behind. Mix on low speed for 30 seconds, increase to medium speed for 30 seconds, and then increase to medium-high speed for 3 minutes, mixing until the dough appears smooth. Don't walk away here—kneading dough is hard work for the mixer and it can bounce right off the counter if you leave it unattended.

3. Spray a large bowl with nonstick cooking spray and transfer the dough to the bowl. Knead for 2 minutes to even out any bumps and lumps. Cover with a damp towel or plastic wrap and set in a warm area to proof until doubled in size, about 1 hour.

4. Turn the dough out onto a lightly floured surface. Divide the dough into three equal pieces. Cover two pieces of dough with a kitchen towel so they won't dry out. With a bench scraper, divide the dough you're working with into three equal pieces and roll each piece into a strand 12 in [30.5 cm] long.

5. Line a baking sheet with parchment paper. Lay all three strands side by side on a lightly floured countertop and pinch them together at the top. Take the right strand and have it jump over the middle strand; it is now the middle strand. Next, take the left strand and have it jump over the middle strand; now it is

the middle strand. Continue the pattern, alternating between right and left, until the strands are braided the whole length. Pinch the bottom of the strands together and place on the prepared baking sheet. Repeat with the remaining two pieces of dough.

6. Whisk together the egg yolks with a pinch of sugar and a pinch of salt. Brush the egg wash over the shaped loaves and sprinkle with 1 Tbsp za'atar per loaf, if using. Let the loaves rise in a warm place until doubled in size, about 30 minutes.

7. While the bread is rising, preheat the oven to 350°F [180°C].

8. Bake until lightly golden, 30 to 35 minutes. Transfer to a rack to cool.

9. To freeze, cool completely before transferring to a resealable storage bag. Frozen challah can be kept in the freezer for up to 2 months. Freshly baked challah can be stored in the fridge for up to 5 days.

FOOD FOR THOUGHT:
This recipe is truly transformative and comforting, and I feel as if I'm channeling my grandmother each time I make it. If you are baking to remember someone or something, surround yourself with reminders of them, such as a picture, or bake with their favorite ingredients.

Upside-Down Pineapple Pound Cake

TOPPING

3 Tbsp unsalted butter

⅓ cup [65 g] packed dark brown sugar

¼ tsp ground cinnamon

Pinch of freshly ground black pepper

Pinch of salt

1 Tbsp whiskey or rum (optional)

1 tsp vanilla extract

1½ cups [255 g] thinly sliced pineapple, cut into 2 in [5 cm] pieces

CAKE

½ cup [100 g] packed dark brown sugar

2 large eggs

1 cup [240 g] sour cream

1 large banana, overripe and mashed

½ cup [120 ml] canola or vegetable oil

1 tsp vanilla extract

½ tsp kosher salt

1½ cups [210 g] all-purpose flour

MAKES 8 SLICES

There's something wholesome about a pound cake. It's sturdy and rich. This pound cake kicks comfort up a notch sweet pineapple—and a hint of alcohol, if added. This cake is just bright enough to comfort you whenever you may need it, one bite at a time.

1. Position a rack in the center of the oven and preheat to 350°F [180°C]. Butter or coat an 8 in [20 cm] square baking dish with nonstick spray. Line the bottom with a square of parchment paper.

TO MAKE THE TOPPING:

1. Add the butter, brown sugar, cinnamon, black pepper, and salt to a medium skillet. Cook the mixture over medium heat, stirring occasionally, until melted and emulsified. Stir in the whiskey or rum, if using, and vanilla. Add the pineapple and bring the mixture to a simmer. Cook for about 5 minutes, turning the pineapple over in the sauce occasionally, until it releases its juices and the mixture thickens to a paste.

2. Pour the mixture into the prepared pan and arrange the pineapple pieces in a single layer.

1 tsp baking powder

¼ tsp baking soda

¼ tsp ground nutmeg

¼ tsp ground ginger

TO MAKE THE CAKE:

1. In a large bowl, whisk the brown sugar and eggs until pale and foamy, about 1 minute. Add the sour cream, mashed banana, oil, vanilla, and salt. Whisk until well combined and smooth. Add the flour, baking powder, baking soda, nutmeg, and ginger to the bowl and whisk until well combined and smooth.

2. Very gently spoon the batter over the pineapple in the prepared pan and smooth the top.

3. Bake the cake until puffed, golden, and a cake tester inserted into the center comes out clean, 35 to 40 minutes. Set the pan on a rack to cool for 10 minutes, then very carefully invert the cake onto a serving plate. Peel off the parchment paper and serve. Store leftovers in the fridge for up to 2 days.

BAKING AFFIRMATION:
Sometimes the world has to flip upside down for me to appreciate all that I have.

Choose Your Own Stud Muffins

BASE MUFFINS

3½ cups [490 g] all-purpose flour

2½ tsp baking powder

½ tsp baking soda

1 tsp salt

¾ cup [180 ml] vegetable oil

3 eggs, at room temperature

1½ cups [300 g] coconut or granulated sugar

¼ cup [50 g] packed light brown sugar

⅔ cup [160 g] Greek yogurt

2 Tbsp whole milk

2 tsp vanilla extract

½ tsp almond extract (optional)

2½ Tbsp turbinado sugar, for sprinkling (optional)

MAKES 16 MUFFINS

My mother always says, "Eat a muffin, look like a muffin." Well, moms aren't always right. These stud muffins are a recipe that I shared on the Food Network and are so easy and fun to make—not to mention they're healthier too! Of course, the beauty is the ability to customize this recipe how you see fit. However you feel that day, you'll be happy this stud muffin is in your life.

TO MAKE THE BASE MUFFINS:

1. Preheat the oven to 350°F [180°C]. Spray two muffin tins with nonstick cooking spray. (You can also use paper muffin liners if you would like, but spray the top of the tin anyway because the muffins are big and spread out.) You will be using only sixteen of the muffin cups.

2. In a large bowl, whisk the flour, baking powder, baking soda, and salt. Set aside.

3. In a separate large bowl, combine the vegetable oil, eggs, coconut or granulated sugar, light brown sugar, Greek yogurt, milk, vanilla, and almond extract (if using) until well mixed.

4. Carefully add the dry ingredients to the wet ingredients and mix well. The batter will be thick. If you are adding mix-ins (see page 124), stir them in now. (If you are making jam muffins, add a dollop of jam to the center of each muffin once the batter is scooped into the muffin tin.)

5. Divide the batter evenly among the sixteen muffin cups, filling each nearly to the top. Sprinkle each with about ½ tsp turbinado sugar (if using). Bake for 25 to 30 minutes, or until golden brown. Let cool completely.

6. Wrap and store at room temperature for up to 3 days or freeze for up to 1 month.

OPTIONAL FLAVOR COMBOS

FRUIT MUFFINS

Mix in ¾ cup [about 95 g] frozen berries, 1 tsp chia seeds or flaxseed, and ½ tsp grated lemon zest, if desired, to the batter in step 4.

CHOCOLATE CHIP MUFFINS

Mix in ½ cup [90 g] white, dark, or milk chocolate chips to the batter in step 4.

CONFETTI MUFFINS

Mix in ¼ cup [70 g] rainbow sprinkles to the batter in step 4.

FOOD FOR THOUGHT:
We all look for comfort in different ways. Don't be afraid to express what you need, whether from yourself or others, in order to heal.

Grandma Peggy's Kanafeh

SYRUP

1 cup [200 g] sugar

1 tsp orange blossom water

1 tsp rose water

PASTRY

2 lb [910 g] part skim or whole-milk ricotta

½ cup [120 ml] heavy cream

⅓ cup [65 g] sugar

2 Tbsp cornstarch

2 tsp rose water

1 tsp orange blossom water

1½ cups [330 g] unsalted butter

One 16 oz [455 g] box kataifi (shredded phyllo dough)

SERVES 8

Listen to me because I mean this: Kanafeh, a shredded phyllo dough and ricotta dessert, is the gateway to all deliciousness. It is the ultimate Middle Eastern dessert, but every person deserves to taste it. My favorite not-so-secret ingredient in this recipe is rose water. Generations of Middle Eastern bakers have been using rose water for its delicate and floral aroma and taste, helping bring balance to the dish. This kanafeh is so comforting to me because it brings me back to my childhood and connects me to my Syrian ancestry.

1. Preheat the oven to 350°F [180°C]. Have a 3 qt [2.8 L] baking dish ready.

TO MAKE THE SYRUP:

1. In a small saucepan over medium heat, whisk together the sugar, ½ cup [120 ml] of water, the orange blossom water, and rose water until the sugar dissolves, then decrease the heat to low and allow it to simmer for 15 minutes, or until the syrup thickens slightly. Pour the syrup into a heat-safe container and refrigerate until ready to use.

TO MAKE THE PASTRY:

1. In a 4 qt [3.8 L] saucepan over medium heat, whisk together the ricotta and heavy cream. Bring the mixture to a gentle boil.

cont.

2. In a medium bowl, whisk together the sugar and cornstarch. Stir it into the ricotta mixture and allow the mixture to return to a gentle boil, then lower the heat to a simmer. Add the rose water and orange blossom water and simmer for 5 minutes more, whisking occasionally. Remove the pan from the heat and let cool.

3. Melt the butter in a small saucepan over low heat. Do not allow it to boil! As the butter melts, tear up the kanafeh into shreds and place in a medium bowl. Pour the melted butter over the kanafeh and toss them together until the kanafeh is completely saturated.

TO ASSEMBLE AND SERVE:

1. Spread half of the kanafeh in the bottom of the baking dish, then top it with all of the ricotta mixture, spreading it evenly. Top with the remaining kanafeh. Bake for 1 hour, or until the top turns golden.

2. Remove from the oven, pour the syrup over the kanafeh, and allow the dish to cool slightly. Scoop servings with a spoon and serve warm. Store the dish, covered in plastic wrap, in the fridge for up to 4 days.

FOOD FOR THOUGHT:
Food often brings back memories from our childhood. Focus on the flavors or what really made that memory special, and see how you can bring those feelings into your life today.

Ka'ak (Round Mediterranean Crackers)

¾ cup plus 1 Tbsp [195 ml] warm water, about 110°F [45°C]

1 tsp active dry yeast

½ tsp sugar

2¾ cups [385 g] all-purpose flour

1 tsp aniseed

1 tsp ground cumin

1 tsp ground coriander

1 tsp table salt

¼ cup [60 ml] extra-virgin olive oil

2 Tbsp unsalted butter, melted

1 egg, beaten

¼ cup [35 g] sesame seeds

MAKES 15 CRACKERS

To me, ka'ak is synonymous with nostalgia. After every holiday meal at Great-Grandma Sarah Benun's house (where everyone was welcome), these cracker-like breads were served with some Turkish coffee while my family sat around the living room. I was too young to drink coffee, but that didn't stop me from dipping the ka'ak into it. The savory flavors mixed with the coffee offer a truly warming bite. But if you want to just snack on them, you can do that too. It's the ultimate noncommittal treat!

1. In a small bowl, combine the water, yeast, and sugar. Set aside for 10 minutes while the yeast activates.

2. In a large bowl, whisk the flour, aniseed, cumin, coriander, and salt. Make a well in the center and add the oil, butter, and yeast mixture. Use a wooden spoon to stir until a dough begins to form, then use your hands to bring everything together and knead the dough just until it becomes elastic, 2 to 3 minutes. Cover the dough with a kitchen towel and allow it to rise in a warm area for 1 hour.

3. Preheat the oven to 350°F [180°C] and line two baking sheets with parchment paper.

4. Punch down the dough and roll it out into a log. Pinch off a piece the size of a golf ball and roll it between your hands until it begins to form a log shape. Then, place it on a flat work surface and use both hands to roll it back and forth, lightly pushing

cont.

outward each time, until an 8 in [20 cm] long, ¼ in [6 mm] thick rope forms. Gently use the dull edge of a knife to make depressions in the top of the dough every ½ in [13 mm] or so. Take one end of the dough rope in each hand and form a circle with the two ends overlapping, making sure that the indentations are facing upward. Place the completed ka'ak ring on the baking sheet. Repeat this step until all the dough has been shaped, being sure to keep it covered with plastic wrap while not working with it.

5. Once all of the rings are made, brush their tops with the beaten egg and sprinkle liberally with the sesame seeds. Bake for 30 minutes.

6. Lower the oven temperature to 250°F [120°C] and transfer the ka'ak to an ovenproof roasting pan with a lid. Just pile them all up; don't worry about spacing. Bake the ka'ak for 2 hours longer, shaking the pan every 30 minutes or so. This will achieve maximum crispiness!

7. Remove the ka'ak from the oven and let cool completely to achieve the best crunch. You can eat these immediately or store them in an airtight container for up to 4 days.

BAKING AFFIRMATION:
I give myself permission to heal on my own terms and in a way that works for me.

Sambusak

(BRAIDED CHEESE PASTRIES)

1 cup [140 g] all-purpose flour

½ cup [80 g] semolina flour

10 Tbsp [150 g] salted butter, at room temperature

½ tsp fine sea salt

¼ cup [60 ml] warm water, about 110°F [45° C]

4 oz [115 g] grated Muenster or mozzarella cheese

2 eggs

Toasted sesame seeds, for garnish

MAKES 15 PASTRIES

Sambusak is a cheesy, delectable staple of the Syrian community. It's also a symbol of the gathering of women. Sambusak is traditionally made by multiple women in the kitchen, usually while their kids are at school. These beautiful homemakers would all come together and laugh as they braided the delicate edges, then serve them to those same children with pride when they trooped in from school.

1. Preheat the oven to 325°F [165°C].

2. In the bowl of a stand mixer fitted with the paddle attachment, or in a medium bowl using a handheld electric mixer, combine the flour, semolina, butter, and salt. Slowly add the water while mixing. The dough will be crumbly.

3. Scoop it all together with your hands and knead until a ball forms. Cover the dough with plastic wrap until ready to use.

4. In a separate bowl, combine the cheese and 1 egg to make the filling.

5. Sprinkle some sesame seeds on a small plate and set a sheet of parchment paper on a baking sheet. Take a walnut-size piece of dough and roll it into a ball. Lightly dip one side of the dough ball into the sesame seeds and place it sesame-side down on the prepared baking sheet. Then, use your palm to

cont.

NOTE: *For an extra flavor boost, incorporate chopped chives into the filling mixture before baking.*

press it flat into a round that is 3 to 4 in [7.5 to 10 cm] in diameter. Spoon a heaping 1 tsp of filling onto the dough and close it into a half-moon shape, using your fingers to seal the edges. For prettier edges, use a fork to create a pattern along the seal. For a traditional crimp, pinch one corner at the end of the crescent and fold the dough toward you. Pinch the little peak it makes and fold it toward you. Keep going until you get to the end of the crescent, and tuck the last part under. Repeat with the remaining dough and filling.

6. Beat the remaining egg and use it to lightly brush the tops of the pastries. Bake for 20 to 25 minutes, or until golden and crisp.

7. Serve immediately for melted cheesy goodness!

FOOD FOR THOUGHT:
It takes a village, as the saying goes. Gathering with friends or family is a good way to get through difficult times, and baking sambusak is a perfect excuse to come together.

Red Velvet Cookies with Cream Cheese Glaze

COOKIES

½ cup [110 g] unsalted butter, at room temperature

¾ cup [150 g] packed light brown sugar

1 egg

¼ cup [60 ml] buttermilk

2 tsp vanilla extract

Red food coloring, to your preference

1½ cups [210 g] all-purpose flour

¼ cup [30 g] unsweetened cocoa powder

1 tsp baking soda

½ tsp table salt

1 cup [180 g] white chocolate chips

GLAZE

1 cup [120 g] powdered sugar

4 oz [115 g] cream cheese, at room temperature

3 Tbsp unsalted butter, at room temperature

1 Tbsp whole milk

2 tsp vanilla extract

MAKES 24 COOKIES

Growing up, red velvet cake was reserved for special occasions like birthdays and holidays. I'd get to pick it out at my favorite local Brooklyn bakery—it felt magical somehow. I was attracted to the color and aroma of the cake. I didn't understand how the warmth of the red hues came to be and assumed it was some type of mystical baking know-how. Imagine my surprise when I learned it was just food coloring! This recipe is a physical manifestation of comfort that's perfectly portioned for sharing with loved ones.

TO MAKE THE COOKIES:

1. In a large bowl, use an electric hand mixer to beat the butter until fluffy.

2. Add the brown sugar to the butter and continue beating until creamed together. Next, add the egg, buttermilk, vanilla, and food coloring. Beat until the food coloring is well distributed, using a rubber spatula to periodically scrape down the sides.

3. Next, add the flour, cocoa powder, baking soda, and salt. Continue to mix on medium speed, scraping down the sides as needed, until everything is well combined.

4. Use the spatula to fold in the chocolate chips. Transfer the cookie dough to the fridge to chill for at least 1 hour.

cont.

TO MAKE THE GLAZE:

1. While the dough chills, add the glaze ingredients to a medium bowl. Using an electric mixer, beat the mixture on medium speed until smooth and fluffy. Cover the glaze and set it aside at room temperature.

TO BAKE AND DECORATE:

1. Once the dough has chilled, preheat the oven to 350°F [180°C]. Line two baking sheets with parchment paper and begin rolling the dough into 2 in [5 cm] balls.

2. Place roughly nine dough balls on each baking sheet, spaced at least 2 in [5 cm] apart, until all the dough is used. Use the heel of your hand to lightly flatten the dough.

3. Bake the cookies for 10 to 12 minutes, or until the edges are set but the middle is still slightly underdone and puffy. Allow them to cool on the pan for 2 to 3 minutes, then transfer to a cooling rack to cool completely.

4. In a small pot over low heat, slightly warm the cream cheese glaze so that it becomes pourable and drizzle over the cookies. You can eat these cookies while the glaze is still gooey or wait about 30 minutes for it to set. Store at room temperature for up to 12 hours or refrigerate for up to 4 days.

BAKING AFFIRMATION:
I acknowledge the changes that have occurred in my life, and I'm grateful for the good.

Challah Caramel Bread Pudding

One 16 oz [455 g] loaf of challah, store-bought or homemade (page 104), cut into 1 in [2.5 cm] cubes

4 cups [960 ml] whole milk

5 eggs

½ cup [100 g] plus 2 Tbsp sugar

2 tsp vanilla extract

2 tsp ground cinnamon

½ tsp ground nutmeg

¼ cup [55 g] salted butter, melted

½ cup [90 g] semisweet chocolate chips

½ cup [120 g] Caramel Sauce (page 32), slightly warmed

SERVES 12

This bread pudding is made using my Madonna-approved challah bread (page 104) that kick-started my baking business, JackBakes. Bread pudding reminds me of having challah French toast growing up—if you only ate the middle (no shame in that). The challah provides the perfect base, absorbing the cinnamon, nutmeg, and vanilla for a rich and decadent bite. The best part? The chocolate chips and caramel drizzle on top! Serve this up at brunch, or save it for dessert.

1. Preheat the oven to 350°F [180°C]. Grease a 9 by 13 in [23 by 33 cm] baking dish with 1 Tbsp coconut oil.

2. Spread the challah cubes on an ungreased baking sheet and toast for 5 minutes.

3. In a large bowl, combine the milk, eggs, ½ cup [100 g] of the sugar, the vanilla, 1 tsp of the cinnamon, and the nutmeg. Be sure to whisk well so that the eggs are completely incorporated.

4. Once the bread is toasted, add it to a separate large bowl and toss together with the remaining 2 Tbsp of sugar, the remaining 1 tsp of cinnamon, and the melted butter.

5. Transfer the toasted bread mixture to the prepared baking dish and sprinkle with the chocolate chips. Pour the custard mixture over the bread. Use your hands to push down any bread sticking above the

custard so that everything is completely saturated. Set aside for at least 15 minutes so the challah can absorb the custard.

6. Bake for 45 minutes, or until the custard is set. Immediately drizzle with the caramel. Allow to cool a bit before serving (if you can wait that long). Store leftovers in the fridge for up to 3 days.

FOOD FOR THOUGHT:
You can't work through something you're still holding on to. Allow yourself to feel what you're feeling, even if that feeling is uncomfortable, and find comfort in the release.

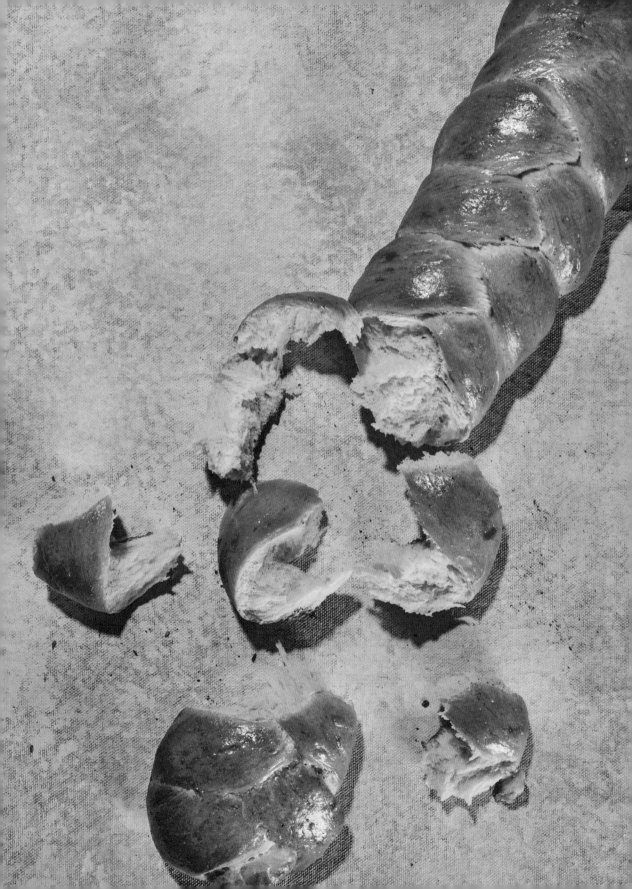

Middle Eastern Rice Pudding

RICE PUDDING

½ cup plus 2 Tbsp [130 g]
long-grain white rice

2 cups [480 ml] whole milk

¼ cup [50 g] sugar

2 tsp vanilla extract

Pinch of table salt

½ tsp rose water (optional)

FOR SERVING

Roasted and salted chopped
pistachios, for garnish

SERVES 6

I remember my grandmother making this recipe when I was a child, specifically when I was around on Saturday evenings. I seemed to be the only rice pudding freak in the family. If you want the best grandmotherly advice on rice pudding, take her words to heart: "You want the best rice pudding? Use cream. You want great rice pudding? Use whole milk. Good? Use 2 percent milk. If you want to use skim milk, just skip the pudding and save the calories!"

This pudding is warm and mushy, every bite just like a hug from Grandma.

TO MAKE THE RICE PUDDING:

1. In a medium, heavy-bottomed saucepan, bring the rice and 2 cups [480 ml] of cold water to a boil. Decrease the heat to a simmer (uncovered) and cook until the rice has absorbed almost all the water, 10 to 15 minutes.

2. Add the milk, mix well, and cook uncovered over low heat for 45 to 60 minutes (the amount of time will depend on the thickness of the pan and heat source), stirring frequently so it doesn't stick to the pan or form a thick film on top. It will bubble and thicken as it cooks. The milk will get absorbed and the grains of rice will appear more prominently. The texture will be rich and custardy.

3. Add the sugar, vanilla, salt, and rose water, if using. Stir well and cook over low heat for an additional 5 minutes.

4. Remove from the heat and allow to cool for 20 to 30 minutes. It will continue to thicken as it cools.

TO SERVE:

1. Serve each scoop with a generous sprinkle of the chopped pistachios. Rice pudding can be served warm, at room temperature, or chilled. Store leftovers in the fridge for up to 3 days.

FOOD FOR THOUGHT:
Healing isn't linear. You might experience that same grief again but from a different perspective, and hopefully you find more comfort each time.

Trifecta of Comfort Ice Cream Sandwiches

COOKIE LAYER

¼ cup [55 g] unsalted butter, at room temperature

¼ cup [50 g] packed light brown sugar

2 Tbsp granulated sugar

½ tsp vanilla extract

1 egg yolk, at room temperature

½ cup plus 2 Tbsp [90 g] all-purpose flour

¼ tsp fine sea salt

¼ tsp baking soda

½ cup [90 g] semisweet chocolate chips or chunks

BROWNIE LAYER

½ cup [100 g] granulated sugar

¼ cup [55 g] unsalted butter, melted but still warm

½ tsp vanilla extract

¼ tsp coffee extract

1 egg white, room temperature

¼ cup [35 g] all-purpose flour

2 Tbsp cocoa powder

MAKES 9 ICE CREAM SANDWICHES

Ice cream makes everything better. But when you combine it with both brownies and cookies? Talk about the ultimate dessert trifecta. And while ice cream won't literally fix our problems, our grief, or our sadness, sometimes we need something (or a few somethings) sweet to help us get through.

1. Coat two 8 by 8 in [20 by 20 cm] baking dishes with nonstick cooking spray and line them both with parchment paper. You want the parchment to extend past the tops of the baking dishes to help lift the sandwich layers later.

TO MAKE THE COOKIE LAYER:

1. In the bowl of a stand mixer fitted with the paddle attachment, or in a medium bowl using a handheld electric mixer, beat the butter, brown sugar, granulated sugar, and vanilla until well combined. Add the egg yolk and beat until smooth, about 1 minute.

2. In a small bowl, whisk the flour, salt, and baking soda. Add the dry ingredients to the butter mixture and mix until combined. Add the chocolate chips and mix until incorporated. With your hands, spread the dough thinly into every corner of one of the prepared baking dishes and set aside.

TO MAKE THE BROWNIE LAYER:

1. In another large bowl, using a stand mixer or hand-held electric mixer, beat the granulated sugar,

¼ tsp baking powder

¼ tsp fine sea salt

ICE CREAM

2½ cups [590 g] your favorite flavor ice cream or gelato (Talenti works well here), softened in the fridge for 20 minutes

butter, vanilla, and coffee extract until well combined. Add the egg white and mix well.

2. In a small bowl, combine the flour, cocoa powder, baking powder, and salt. Add the dry ingredients to the butter mixture and whisk until combined. Spread the brownie batter in a thin layer in the other prepared baking dish and spread into an even layer.

TO BAKE AND ASSEMBLE:

1. Preheat the oven to 325°F [165°C].

2. Bake both pans on the same middle rack until the edges start to brown and pull away from sides of the pans, about 15 minutes for the brownie layer and 20 minutes for the cookie layer.

3. Let cool completely on a cooling rack. When cool, gently loosen the edges with a knife or thin metal spatula and then pop them in the freezer for 20 minutes.

4. Remove the cookie and brownie layers from the freezer and take them out of their pans. Flip the brownie layer upside down and place in one of the baking pans, reusing the parchment. Scoop the softened ice cream onto the brownie to cover and smooth it out. Top it with the cookie half.

5. Cover in plastic wrap and freeze for at least 4 hours. When ready to serve, run a knife around the edges of the pan. Remove and cut into nine equal pieces. Serve immediately or store, tightly wrapped in wax paper, in the freezer for up to 2 months.

Dealing with Stress an

Anxiety

Let me tell you, writing a cookbook is stressful. I will admit, I had questions running nonstop through my mind. "Will this *specific* chapter make sense?" (It does.) "Will these recipes be delicious and easy to follow?" (They are.) As I continued to write, I became anxious. "Is it all going to come together in the time line? Is this going to turn out the way I want?" (Yes, and yes.)

Our bodies communicate to us through stressful and anxious feelings and/or sensations. We sometimes think of those feelings as interchangeable, but you should know there is a difference between stress and anxiety.

Anxiety is rooted in uncertainty around the unknown, whether it's related to something from our past or an unseen event in our future. Stress is a reaction to a given situation in *that* moment, and it affects our confidence in our ability to handle it. Anxiety says, "I can't understand what happened/is going to happen," whereas stress says, "I can't handle this." Can you imagine what would happen if both occurred at the same time!? Oy vey!

It's important to also understand what our responses can be. If you're like me, you might go into overdrive—you feel the adrenaline rushing through your veins. I get shaky. I bite my nails. Or maybe your stomach starts to act up, which is not a pleasant feeling, or you go the opposite route and numb the feelings with stress eating—like reaching your hand into the cookie jar to stuff your face with Double Stuf Oreos and almond milk (that might just be me).

Let's talk for a moment about the kinds of stress we experience: lowercase *s* stress and uppercase *S* Stress. Lowercase *s* stressors are the smaller things outside of our control like, "Ugh, I can't find a parking spot." (If you've ever lived in NYC, you know that feeling all too well.) On the other hand, uppercase *S* Stressors are the STRESSFUL things in life. These are the moments that challenge our expectations of how things are going to go, things that may be life-altering in big and difficult ways.

One uppercase *S* Stress moment for me was the time I was fired, by my dad, from my job in the family business selling *schmattas* (Yiddish for "fabrics") in the Garment District.

I felt like the rug had been pulled out from under me, and I was suddenly left to figure out where I was going and what I wanted to do next. This big life change that I did not expect, or necessarily want, pushed me— along with my Aunt Dina's encouragement—to attend NYU to become a licensed psychotherapist. You can only imagine how stressed and anxious I became now that I had no source of income AND I had to pay for rent. One day, a light bulb went off—my challah bread! It was always a winner at Shabbat meals. I decided to start selling my baked goods as a side hustle, and that's how my friend, Rudy Espinoza, helped me launch my baking company, JackBakes. I sold my challah throughout grad school to make the extra money I needed to support myself and my future career. Baking was my way to handle the stress.

If it hadn't been for those two uppercase *S* Stress moments in my life, I wouldn't be here with my Baking Therapy approach and cookbook (so thanks, Dad!). What I'm trying to say is that stress doesn't have to be seen as a negative. In fact, stress can be positive; by working through it, we end up in a better place than where we started.

There's a difference between dealing with your problems and coping with them (ahem, stress eating), but we need to feel our way through stress and anxiety, not ignore it. It pays to lean into these moments and really listen to the things they're stirring up in us. When you're faced with a stressful situation and you're having that familiar anxious feeling, think to yourself, "Where do I feel the stress? How do I feel this anxious feeling?" As much as we—as humans—want to move away from uncomfortable feelings, they're actually designed to help us recognize pain points.

I often ask my patients what triggers their stress and anxiety. If we're talking around November and December, they tell me "the holidays," without fail. I refer to that time period as "three full days of Jewish guilt." Is it any coincidence that we're baking more during November and December? No, my dear!

Baking is a foolproof way to combat stress and anxiety; it's why Baking Therapy exists! It serves up an alternative to trying to numb the bad feelings and allows us to channel that energy into creation. In other words, we're getting out of our heads and into our hands.

Believe it not, therapists also get stressed! But a stress ball doesn't really belong in the kitchen. Thankfully, the technique of kneading dough gives us the same relief as squeezing a stress ball. Plus, you get to enjoy a gorgeous treat once it's fully baked. Talk about a win-win.

Sift the flour. Measure the sugar. Crack that egg. All these baking techniques can help reduce stress. Why? Because they're small, easily accomplished steps that put you in control. For me, Mr. Control Freak, I turn to baking for that sense of certainty. So repeat after me: Baking does not have to be stressful!

Stress baking on the other hand? That's where some real healing can begin. It might seem daunting—a marathon of baking—but just remember what my Aunt Dina always says: "Hey, just focus on putting one foot in front of the other." If you follow all the instructions, it should turn out pretty close to the way it is described. As you complete some tasks, celebrate those accomplishments. It's like crossing off an item on your never-ending to-do list. Go you!

Feel free to share those accomplishments—and treats—with others, especially after stress baking. For starters, baking for someone else is a small token to show you care. It gives you a chance to sit down and catch up too, which can help alleviate some stressful feelings. I've found it's always helpful to talk through what I'm experiencing.

Baking Therapy is more than the techniques or following the steps of a recipe. It also comes down to what we're baking. Are you using healthier ingredients? Or functional ingredients? Are you baking something good for you or good to you? (Reread that last question.)

Functional ingredients help your body function and create a better state of mind. Lavender possesses a calming aroma (it's one of my favorites). Ginger can help settle an upset stomach. And yes, even something sweet can make a bitter day all better. What I'm saying is, the quality of the ingredients we put into our bodies can be reflective of the value we place on ourselves.

A word to the wise: Everything in moderation, even moderation. If the road is getting a little rocky, it's OK to reach for a little rocky road ice cream. It'll be a yummy, quick treat to lessen the stressful feelings. And before you go popping that Xanax (as a reminder, you need a doctor's prescription), try out one of these stress-less recipes.

Quick Session
HOW DO LOBSTERS GROW?

One of the top problems my patients talk about is their crippling anxiety. Sometimes it's reality and sometimes it's just venting. It feels good to let out what's causing us stress. But as I tell them, no kvetching!

I had a patient who kept repeating "I have anxiety" over and over. *Anxiety* is such an overarching term that, to get to the root of it, I had to ask, "What's behind the anxiety?" For him (and if I'm being honest, me too), it was about change. He didn't know how to embrace change. Well, what was the anxiety trying to tell him? Either numb it out (not the healthiest) or go through it. As Winston Churchill once said, "If you're going through hell, keep going."

I shared with him one of Rabbi Dr. Abraham Twerski's talks on stress and anxiety with lobsters as the subject. (And no, it's not about how good they taste slathered in butter.) On the inside, lobsters are soft, mushy animals, but they have a rigid exterior shell. That shell does not grow as the lobster grows, causing it to become uncomfortable. So, what does the lobster do? Instead of trying to force the shell to change, the lobster goes under a rock and casts off that shell. A new shell is produced, and eventually that one will get to be uncomfortable as well. The lobster repeats the cycle of casting off the old and producing a new shell.

The key here is the stimulus, or the event: For the lobster to be able to grow, it has to feel uncomfortable. The same goes for my patients—and for you. The discomfort from stress and anxiety is trying to help us grow. It's an opportunity to acknowledge the moment, take some time to go through it, and cast off the emotional weight. Whatever it is you're going through, do just that. Go through it. And just remember, what would a lobster do?

Chocolate Chip Babka Crunch

BREAD

½ cup [120 ml] warm water, about 110°F [45°C]

3½ tsp active dry yeast

¾ cup [150 g] plus 2 tsp sugar, plus a pinch for the egg wash

4½ cups [630 g] bread flour

1½ tsp table salt, plus a pinch for the egg wash

¼ cup [55 g] unsalted butter, melted

1 egg

1 tsp honey

2 tsp vanilla extract

1 egg yolk

1 cup [180 g] semisweet chocolate chips

CRUMB

¼ cup [55 g] salted butter, at room temperature

½ cup [100 g] sugar

½ tsp vanilla extract

½ cup [70 g] all-purpose flour

¼ cup [45 g] chocolate chips

SERVES 6

I don't know whether I have made this clear: I love a good crumb. More than I know how to express in words. My next baking book will probably have a recipe that is just a big pan of crumb topping (kidding, I think). My Chocolate Chip Babka Crunch is the best of both worlds: It's bread and dessert, all at once! The knots are super simple but lend a sophisticated air to this scrumptious dessert. It also freezes beautifully, so feel free to double the recipe.

TO MAKE THE BREAD:

1. In a small bowl, combine the warm water, yeast, and 2 tsp of the sugar. Set aside for 10 minutes while the yeast activates.

2. In a large bowl, whisk together the remaining ¾ cup [150 g] sugar, the bread flour, and salt. Add the melted butter, egg, honey, vanilla, and ½ cup plus 2 Tbsp [150 ml] water. Use a wooden spoon to just combine the ingredients, then pour in the yeast mixture. Continue mixing until you have a mostly combined and workable dough.

3. Turn out the dough onto a lightly floured surface and knead for 5 to 8 minutes, or until the dough is smooth and elastic. Spray a large bowl with nonstick cooking spray and set the dough inside.

4. In a small bowl, whisk the egg yolk and a pinch each of sugar and salt to form an egg wash. Use a pastry brush to brush the entire surface of the dough. Reserve the remaining egg wash. Cover with

cont.

plastic wrap and allow the dough to rise in a warm place for about 1 hour or until it has doubled in size.

5. Punch down the risen dough and cut it into six equal pieces. Roll each piece into a 12 in [30.5 cm] long strand and use your fingers to sprinkle 2 to 3 Tbsp of chocolate chips down each strand, pinching the dough over them as you go. This will create a gooey chocolate center.

6. Coat a 9 in [23 cm] round pan with nonstick cooking spray and begin forming the dough into knots. Simply grab each end of each strand, tie it into a knot, and pinch the ends together, tucking them underneath the knot.

7. Place the knots in the pan in a flower shape, with one knot in the middle and five knots spread in a circle around it. The dough will touch and that's OK!

8. Brush the entire surface with the egg wash once more, reserving any remaining egg wash. Cover the babka with plastic wrap and let rise a second time for 1 hour. Brush it with the egg wash one more time.

9. Preheat the oven to 350°F [180°C].

TO MAKE THE CRUMB:

1. Place the butter, sugar, and vanilla in a small bowl. Use your fingers to incorporate the butter and create a nice crumbly texture with the sugar. Add the flour and continue working the mixture, using your fingers

cont.

in a pinching motion. Sprinkle the crumb over the babka dough, making sure to get it into the crevices as well. Add chocolate chips on top of the crumb. Don't be afraid of a thick crumb. It's your friend!

TO BAKE AND SERVE:

1. Bake the babka for 35 to 40 minutes, or until it is a lovely golden brown on top. Remove from the oven and allow to cool slightly, but be sure to eat it while it's still warm.

2. Babka can be stored in an airtight container in the freezer for up to 2 months.

FOOD FOR THOUGHT:
Times of stress can be times of growth (if you allow them to be).

Not-Your-Ordinary Blackberry Cobbler

6 cups [720 g] blackberries, fresh or thawed if frozen

⅔ cup [130 g] plus 3 Tbsp granulated sugar

3 Tbsp cornstarch

1 Tbsp fresh lemon juice

1½ cups [210 g] all-purpose flour

1½ tsp baking powder

½ tsp kosher salt

½ tsp ground cinnamon

¼ cup [55 g] cold salted vegan butter substitute

¾ cup [180 ml] soy milk or nondairy milk of choice

1 tsp vanilla extract

Turbinado sugar, for garnish

Dairy-free/vegan vanilla ice cream, for serving

SERVES 8

Cobblers are an "all-around" dessert. And they're simple to make, too: You just need a wooden spoon, a measuring cup, and a bowl. On those long, stressful days when you just want to put your feet up, use this delightfully vegan recipe to set it and forget it. Take the hour baking time to unwind with one of your favorite shows or whip up dinner knowing that a yummy dessert will be waiting for you when you're done. Plus, this recipe uses cinnamon to add an extra bit of warmth and comfort to your senses. Pair the hot cobbler with cold vanilla bean ice cream and you'll be in instant heaven!

1. Preheat the oven to 375°F [190°C]. Grease an 8 in [20 cm] square baking pan with nonstick cooking spray and set aside.

2. In a large mixing bowl, add the blackberries, ⅔ cup of the granulated sugar, the cornstarch, and lemon juice. Stir gently to combine and set aside while you prepare the topping.

3. In another large mixing bowl, whisk together the flour, baking powder, salt, and cinnamon until combined. Cut the cold vegan butter into small cubes and add to the flour mixture. With your fingertips, pinch and rub the vegan butter into the flour mixture until coarse crumbs form and the butter is evenly distributed.

cont.

NOTE: *Feel free to adjust the amount of sugar in the blackberry filling to your taste; sour, under-ripe berries may need more sugar, while sweet, ripe berries may need a little less.*

4. Add the soy milk and vanilla to the butter mixture and fold with a silicone spatula until just combined.

5. Pour the berries into the prepared baking pan. Using an ice cream scoop or ¼ cup [60 ml] measuring cup, scoop dollops of batter over the blackberries. Sprinkle turbinado sugar over the batter.

6. Bake for 30 to 35 minutes, or until the topping is golden and the filling is bubbling. Let stand for 10 minutes before serving warm with vegan vanilla ice cream. Store leftovers in the fridge for up to 2 days.

BAKING AFFIRMATION:
Today I trust that things will work out for me, even though I may not be able to see that right now.

Feelin' Peachy Galette

WITH CARDAMOM

CRUST

1½ cups [210 g] all-purpose flour

2 tsp granulated sugar

½ tsp table salt

½ cup [110 g] very cold unsalted butter, thinly sliced

½ cup [120 ml] ice water

1 egg plus 1 tsp water for egg wash

FILLING

2 lb [910 g] fresh peaches, peeled, pitted, and thinly sliced

1½ Tbsp fresh lemon juice

½ cup [100 g] plus 1 tsp granulated sugar

1 tsp cornstarch

1 tsp vanilla extract

1 tsp ground cardamom

TOPPINGS

Demerara sugar, for sprinkling

Homemade Whipped Cream (page 39)

SERVES 6

A galette is a rustic tart with almost no rules. It is meant to be ruggedly shaped and look like it belongs on the dining table of a cabin. So, when you fold the crust over the spiced peaches, be forgiving with yourself. No matter how this tart turns out in the end, it will turn out the way it was supposed to. Imperfect can be perfect, just like you.

TO MAKE THE CRUST:

1. In a medium bowl, whisk together the flour, granulated sugar, and salt. Add the sliced butter and use a handheld pastry blender or fork to cut in the butter and form a crumbly dough. Add the ice water, a little at a time, using a wooden spoon to stir the dough together. Use your hands to quickly form the dough into a 1 in [2.5 cm] thick flat disk. You want to be quick so that the butter doesn't begin to melt. Wrap it in plastic wrap and chill in the fridge for 30 minutes.

2. Preheat the oven to 400°F [200°C] and line a baking sheet with parchment paper.

TO MAKE THE FILLING:

1. While the dough chills, in a medium bowl, combine the peaches, lemon juice, and 1 tsp of the granulated sugar. Set aside for 10 minutes.

2. Drain off any excess liquid from the peaches that has accumulated in the bottom of the bowl. Add the cornstarch, remaining ½ cup [100 g] granulated

cont.

sugar, vanilla, and cardamom. Toss the fruit to combine well.

TO ASSEMBLE AND BAKE:

1. Remove the dough from the fridge and lightly
    flour a work surface. Flour a rolling pin and roll
    the dough to about ¼ in [6 mm] thickness. Aim for
    a circular shape, but don't stress too much. The
    beauty of a galette is that it isn't supposed to be
    shaped perfectly!

2. Using your rolling pin, roll up the dough and transfer
    it to the prepared baking sheet.

3. Spoon the fruit onto the pie crust, leaving at least
    a 2 in [5 cm] border all around. Then, fold the crust
    over the fruit, leaving the middle exposed. Whisk
    together the egg wash and use a pastry brush to
    coat the exposed edges of the crust.

4. Bake for 35 minutes, or until the crust is golden
    brown. Remove the galette from the oven and
    allow it to cool.

TO TOP AND SERVE:

1. Sprinkle the galette with demerara sugar and serve
    with whipped cream. Store leftovers in the fridge for
    up to 2 days.

FOOD FOR THOUGHT:
Think of stress like preheating
the oven: You'll get hot quickly,
but once you're done with the
experience, you'll cool down.

No-Bake Cashew "Cheesecake"

3 cups [420 g] raw cashews

1½ cups [210 g] raw almonds

¼ tsp fine sea salt, plus a pinch for the crust

2 cups [300 g] pitted Medjool dates

2½ tsp vanilla extract

⅔ cup [145 g] coconut oil, melted

½ cup [120 ml] plus 1 tsp agave nectar

4 Tbsp fresh lemon juice

2 cups [240 g] strawberries (fresh or thawed if frozen)

1 tsp chia seeds

SERVES 10

My sister Margaux is a powerhouse in the kitchen. As a registered dietitian and nutritionist whose mentality is stick to whole foods, not diet fads, her philosophy pairs science with enjoying food, balancing flavor with health. She is also a fuss-free foodie! Trust me, this no-bake cheesecake recipe of hers is just that. Make this cheesecake when you are feeling like a decadent treat without a ton of work. Sit back, relax, and reclaim your time and health with her dairy-free recipe. (Note: This is an overnight recipe.)

1. Place the raw cashews in a large bowl and fill the bowl with cold water. Soak overnight. (You can soak them for as little as 2 to 3 hours, but if you wait overnight, the cheesecake will be creamier.)

2. Line a 9 in [23 cm] springform pan with a circular piece of parchment paper and set aside.

3. Place the almonds and a pinch of the sea salt in a food processor and process until you see medium-size chunks of almond. Add the dates and ½ tsp of the vanilla and process until the pieces are small, uniform, and stick together when you squeeze a tiny bit between your fingers. Pour the crust mixture into the prepared pan and press it down evenly with a glass or your palm. Put it in the freezer to firm up for at least 30 minutes.

4. Drain the soaked cashews and put them in the bowl of a blender or food processor (I like using

a high-powered blender like a Vitamix). Add the coconut oil, ½ cup [120 ml] of the agave, 3 Tbsp of the lemon juice, the remaining 2 tsp of vanilla, and the remaining ¼ tsp of sea salt and blend on high speed until smooth. Remove about half of the filling and layer that into the springform pan. Use an offset spatula to smooth and even it out. Place the pan back in the freezer to set for 30 minutes.

5. Meanwhile, add half the strawberries to the remaining filling, process until smooth, and set the blender carafe in the fridge for 30 minutes to chill. Before adding it to the first layer, give it one more whirl in the blender to ensure everything is mixed evenly. Pour the strawberry layer on top of the cheesecake and freeze for an additional 30 minutes.

6. While the cheesecake is setting in the freezer, slice the remaining strawberries and add them to a medium bowl with the remaining 1 Tbsp lemon juice, the remaining 1 tsp of agave, and the chia seeds Set aside for 5 minutes to allow the chia seeds to plump up.

7. Pour the topping over the cheesecake and put it in the fridge for at least 2 hours to set and firm up.

8. When ready to serve, dip a knife in a cup of hot water and slice the cake, wiping the knife dry between each slice. Serve frozen or let thaw for 15 minutes before serving. The thawing makes it a bit softer and easier to slice.

9. Store in the fridge for up to 4 days or the freezer for up to 2 weeks.

FOOD FOR THOUGHT:
Worrying is a down payment on a problem you may never have.

Five-Star Meringue Birthday Cake

DRIED PINEAPPLE FLOWER DECORATIONS

1 whole pineapple

SPONGE CAKE

4 eggs, at room temperature

⅔ cup [130 g] sugar

1 cup [140 g] all-purpose flour

PASTRY CREAM

1 cup [240 ml] whole milk

2 Tbsp sweetened condensed coconut milk

¼ cup [15 g] sweetened shredded coconut

½ tsp vanilla extract

2 egg yolks

2 Tbsp sugar

1½ tsp cornstarch

Pinch of fine sea salt

½ cup [120 ml] heavy cream

MERINGUE

4 egg whites (about ½ cup [120 ml])

1 cup [200 g] sugar

⅛ tsp coconut extract/flavoring

SERVES 12

This is my sister Raquel's favorite cake, inspired by her favorite NYC restaurant. Airy and light, yet somehow moist, this delicately sweet cake is beautiful enough for a wedding and easy enough for a weekend dessert.

TO MAKE THE PINEAPPLE DECORATIONS:

1. Preheat the oven to 200°F [95°C] and line a baking sheet with parchment paper.

2. Using a sharp knife, remove the outer skin of the pineapple and cut the fruit into very thin slices cross-wise (you should be able to see through the slices). Do not remove the core. Arrange the slices in a single layer on the prepared baking sheet and bake for 3 hours, flipping every 30 minutes, or until they are dry and look like flowers with petals.

3. Remove from the oven. If you want flat flowers, let them cool and dry on a parchment-lined cooling rack. If you want the flowers to be three-dimensional, put the warm slices of dried pineapple in metal muffin tins until cool.

TO MAKE THE CAKE:

1. Preheat the oven to 350°F [180°C]. Coat an 8 in [20 cm] round cake pan with nonstick cooking spray and set aside.

2. In the bowl of a stand mixer fitted with the paddle attachment, or in a medium bowl using a handheld

cont.

electric mixer, slowly beat the eggs and sugar until pale yellow and the volume increases, 3 to 4 minutes.

3. Carefully fold in the flour, being careful not to deflate the batter too much.

4. Pour the batter into the prepared pan and bake for 20 to 25 minutes, or until golden brown. It will spring back against your finger when you test it. Set aside to cool.

TO MAKE THE PASTRY CREAM AND ASSEMBLE:

1. While the cake is cooling, in a medium saucepan over medium heat, combine the milk, condensed coconut milk, shredded coconut, and vanilla and bring to a simmer. Remove from the heat and let steep for 45 minutes.

2. In the bowl of a stand mixer fitted with the paddle attachment, or using a medium bowl and handheld electric mixer, combine the egg yolks, sugar, corn-starch, and salt and beat on medium-high speed for about 5 minutes, until it is thick and pale. Gently reheat the milk mixture. With the mixer on low speed, slowly pour in the milk mixture. Transfer back to the saucepan and cook over medium-low heat for about 4 minutes, until bubbles are popping on the surface. Strain through a strainer to remove the coconut. Let cool completely.

3. In the bowl of a stand mixer fitted with the whisk attachment, or in a medium bowl using a handheld

electric mixer, whip the heavy cream until soft peaks form. Add ½ cup [120 ml] of the cooled coconut pastry cream and whip until light and fluffy. You will have about ¼ cup [60 ml] of pastry cream left over; save for another recipe or eat it with a spoon—chef's treat!

4. Using a serrated knife, cut the cake horizontally into three equal layers. Place one layer on a cake stand. Spread with half of the cream and then top with the second layer of cake. Spread with the remaining cream and then top with the third layer of cake. Chill in the fridge while you make the meringue.

TO MAKE THE MERINGUE:

1. In a medium saucepan, bring 1½ in [4 cm] of water to a simmer. In the bowl of a stand mixer fitted with the whisk attachment, or in a metal or glass bowl using a handheld electric mixer, whisk the egg whites, sugar, and coconut extract and then place the bowl over the simmering water. Stir until the mixture reaches 160°F [70°C] on a candy thermometer. Fit the bowl back onto the mixer, or use a handheld electric mixer to beat the mixture until stiff peaks form.

TO TOP AND SERVE:

1. Spread the meringue all over the surface of the cake. Torch the cake to brown it in spots (see Note). To add the pineapple petals, place them in whatever pattern and with as many as you prefer. Be creative! Store leftovers in the fridge for up to 2 days.

Stress-less Banana Pudding Trifle

1 cup [200 g] granulated sugar

¼ cup [35 g] cornstarch

4 egg yolks

3½ cups [840 ml] whole milk

1½ cups [360 ml] heavy cream

½ tsp fine sea salt

Pinch of ground cinnamon

2 Tbsp unsalted butter

1 Tbsp vanilla extract

1 tsp vanilla bean paste

6 or 7 large underripe bananas, peeled and sliced (see Note)

About 44 vanilla wafer cookies (a little more than half a box of Nilla Wafers), plus extra for decorating

2 Tbsp powdered sugar

SERVES 6

It doesn't take a pastry chef to make a trifle; the work is practically done for you. It's impossible to mess up. Just dump the ingredients in a bowl, preferably in aesthetically pleasing layers—but you do you, my dear. This recipe is so nonstressful that you can throw it together at a moment's notice. Did you forget about that dinner party you agreed to go to tonight? No problem. Whip up this trifle in the morning, let it set in the fridge, and then head out the door!

1. In a large bowl, whisk ¼ cup [50 g] of the granulated sugar, the cornstarch, and egg yolks.

2. In a medium saucepan, combine the milk, ½ cup [120 ml] of the heavy cream, the remaining ¾ cup [150 g] of granulated sugar, the sea salt, and cinnamon and bring to a simmer over medium heat. Remove the heated milk from the stove, and using a ladle, slowly add a spoonful of the hot milk into the egg mixture, whisking constantly to prevent the eggs from cooking (this is called tempering). Repeat with a few move ladlefuls, until the outside of the bowl is warm to the touch. Carefully pour the mixture back into the saucepan and bring to a boil. Boil, whisking constantly, for 3 minutes, or until thickened. Remove from the heat and stir in the butter, vanilla, and vanilla paste. Set aside for 15 minutes to cool slightly.

cont.

NOTE: *Use underripe bananas here (slightly green on the end, with no black spots). Don't cut them all up at once—as you layer, you may realize you need not need all of them. It's OK to use store-bought whipped cream if it relieves stress (no judgment here). Keep the pudding covered tightly; if it is exposed to air, the bananas will brown.*

3. Spread ½ cup [120 g] of the pudding in a 9 in [23 cm] clear square baking dish. (I use a Pyrex baking dish but you can make individual portions in stemless wineglasses or double the recipe and use a glass trifle dish.) Add one-third of the sliced bananas in an even layer. Add half the cookies in an even layer and then spread 1 cup [240 ml] of the pudding on top. Add half of the remaining bananas, then another 1 cup [240 ml] of pudding, and then top with the remaining bananas. Top with the remaining cookies and remaining pudding. Cover tightly with plastic wrap and refrigerate for at least 6 hours and up to overnight. (Letting it set overnight is what makes it taste so wonderful—the bananas magically ripen a little bit and the cookies soften so it is one consistent texture.)

4. When ready to serve, beat the remaining 1 cup [240 ml] of heavy cream and the powdered sugar until stiff peaks form. Spread on top of the triffle and then decorate with the extra cookies, crushing some for crumbs and placing some whole ones on top. Store leftovers in the fridge in an airtight container for up to 2 days.

BAKING AFFIRMATION:
Today, I will let go of expectations and allow myself to be open to the journey.

Chocolate-Hazelnut Mousse Pie

CRUST

1⅓ cups [185 g] all-purpose flour

½ cup [60 g] powdered sugar

¼ tsp fine sea salt

½ cup [110 g] unsalted butter, cut into small chunks

1 egg yolk

½ tsp vanilla extract

MOUSSE

2 egg whites

1 Tbsp granulated sugar

2 cups [480 ml] heavy cream

1¼ cups [350 g] chocolate-hazelnut spread

¼ tsp instant coffee granules

1 tsp cocoa powder

STRIPE MIXTURES

1 cup [120 g] powdered sugar

1 Tbsp cocoa powder

2 to 3 tsp whole milk

SERVES 8

I took time away from New York to go on a little self-discovery trip. I stopped in Rio on my last day before going back home. I was feeling anxious; I had been on this amazing trip where I had gotten to meet myself away from everything I knew, but now it was time to head home and face my life. I stumbled past a beautiful little bake shop and almost didn't notice a stunning chocolate pie in the window—I was too wrapped up in my thoughts. But I went in and got a piece. It was fluffy, decadent, and so lovely. The slice was covered in a web-like white chocolate drizzle. Up close, the lines looked imperfect. But taking a step back showed me how the whole design worked. And that's what makes this pie so special. No matter how extra the tiny little details look, the bigger picture looks wonderful.

TO MAKE THE CRUST:

1. Preheat the oven to 350°F [180°C]. Have ready an 8 in [20 cm] square metal tart pan with a removable bottom. (You can substitute a round or rectangular pan that is around the same size if you don't have a square one.)

2. In the bowl of a food processor, pulse the flour, powdered sugar, and salt a few times to combine.

3. Add the small chunks of butter and pulse a few times until the butter is in smaller pieces and each piece is covered with flour. Add the egg yolk and vanilla and pulse a few more times until it forms coarse crumbs.

cont.

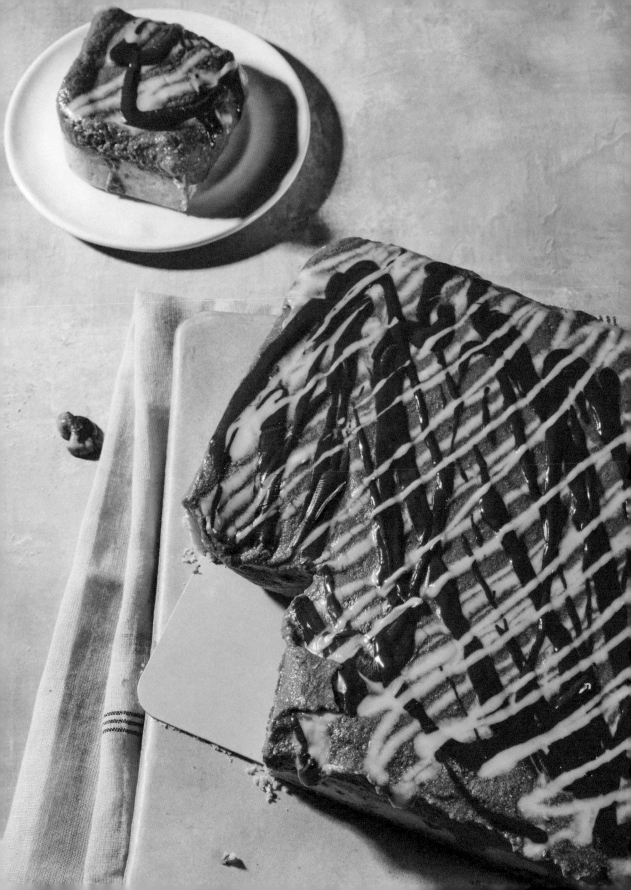

4. Pour the mixture into the tart pan and press it evenly into the bottom and up the sides with a glass or your palm. Place in the freezer for 20 minutes.

5. Cover the crust in aluminum foil (shiny-side down), pressing down over the entire crust (feel free to weigh the foil down with pie weights or dry beans on top), and place the tart pan on a baking sheet. Bake for 15 minutes, then remove the foil and bake for another 10 to 12 minutes, until fully baked and golden brown. Set aside to cool.

TO MAKE THE MOUSSE:

1. While the crust is cooling, in the bowl of a stand mixer fitted with the whisk attachment, or in a medium bowl using a handheld electric mixer, beat the egg whites until soft peaks form. Add the granulated sugar and whisk until stiff peaks form. Set aside.

2. Using a separate clean bowl and the stand mixer or handheld electric mixer, beat the heavy cream until soft peaks form. Add the chocolate-hazelnut spread, coffee granules, and cocoa powder and beat on medium-high speed to incorporate. Gently fold the egg white mixture into the cream mixture.

3. Pour the mousse filling into the cooled tart crust and spread evenly with an offset spatula. Set aside at room temperature while you make the stripes.

cont.

NOTE: *The mousse looks light and fluffy in the mixer but becomes richer when it sits in the fridge. If you have concerns about using raw eggs, you can use pasteurized egg whites instead. It is OK to use store-bought tart dough—in the scheme of things, it doesn't matter and will taste just as good.*

FOOD FOR THOUGHT:
Don't stress about perfection. Allow yourself to zoom out of the situation and see the full picture—not just in the pie but in your own life too. I bet it looks better than your mind led you to believe!

TO MAKE THE STRIPE MIXTURES:

1. Divide the powdered sugar between two bowls. Add the cocoa powder to one bowl. Divide the milk between both bowls and whisk until each mixture is thick yet pourable.

2. Using two piping bags with a narrow tip or two zip-top plastic bags with the tip cut off, pipe zigzags of the white and brown mixtures, creating overlaying stripes. Chill in the fridge for at least 4 hours to set.

TO SERVE:

1. When ready to serve, slice with a sharp knife warmed in hot water to get a clean, bakery-like slice. Store leftovers in the fridge for up to 2 days.

Sicilian Orange Semolina Cake

Grated zest of 3 oranges

¾ cup [150 g] granulated sugar

2 eggs

1 cup [240 g] Greek yogurt

¾ cup [180 ml] olive oil

6 Tbsp [90 ml] fresh orange juice

1½ cups [210 g] all-purpose flour

½ cup [80 g] semolina flour

¾ tsp fine sea salt

1½ tsp baking powder

¼ tsp baking soda

1 cup [115 g] Homemade Whipped Cream (page 39), for topping

⅛ tsp orange blossom water

> **FOOD FOR THOUGHT:**
> Remind yourself how you got here: choice, by choice, by choice. If your choices got you here, your choices can get you out.

SERVES 8

Let's be honest: We all need to calm down sometimes. This cake's fresh and bright citrus scent will help calm your mind.

1. Preheat the oven to 350°F [180°C]. Coat a 9 in [23 cm] round cake pan with nonstick cooking spray, line it with parchment, and then spray the parchment. Set it aside.

2. In a large bowl, massage 2 Tbsp of the orange zest into the sugar with your fingers. Add the eggs and whisk until pale and foamy. Add the yogurt, oil, and orange juice. Whisk vigorously until well combined. Add the all-purpose flour, semolina, salt, baking powder, and baking soda. Whisk until smooth.

3. Pour the batter into the prepared pan, tap it on the counter to release any air pockets, and smooth the surface. Bake the cake until golden brown and the center wobbles gently, 30 to 40 minutes. Let cool in the pan for 30 minutes and then turn out onto a cooling rack and let cool for 2 hours.

4. When ready to serve, in a small bowl, gently mix the whipped cream with the orange blossom water. Dollop and spread the orange blossom whipped cream on top of the cake using an offset spatula and sprinkle the remaining orange zest on top.

5. This cake can keep for about 3 days (without the whipped cream topping), tightly wrapped at room temperature.

Vanilla Bean Panna Cotta

WITH CHOCOLATE SAUCE

PANNA COTTA

One ¼ oz [7 g] packet
unflavored gelatin (2¼ tsp)

3 cups [720 ml] heavy cream

½ cup [100 g] sugar

1 Tbsp vanilla bean paste or
scraped seeds from 1 vanilla bean

CHOCOLATE SAUCE

4 oz [115 g] dark chocolate, chopped

¼ cup [60 ml] heavy cream

2 Tbsp unsalted butter

2 tsp orange zest

1 tsp orange blossom water

Pinch of salt

1 tsp orange zest or calendula
flowers, for garnish

SERVES 6

I've been going to Bar Pitti in NYC since I was young. It's no secret it's my favorite restaurant. I feel like I'm back in Italy whenever I'm there. I always order too much and overeat every time I go. They have a simple panna cotta with chocolate sauce on their dessert menu that is the perfect lightly sweet ending to a heavy meal. This recipe is my homage to Bar Pitti and their panna cotta. This dessert looks fancier and more complicated than it really is, so you'll feel like a baking champion after making it.

1. Place 6 ramekins or stemless wineglasses on a baking sheet and set aside.

TO MAKE THE PANNA COTTA:

1. Pour 2 Tbsp water into a small bowl, sprinkle the gelatin over the top, and let stand for 5 minutes, or until the gelatin softens.

2. Meanwhile, in a medium saucepan over medium-low heat, combine the heavy cream, sugar, and vanilla bean paste and simmer for 5 minutes. Remove from the heat.

3. Add the gelatin mixture to the hot cream mixture and stir until the gelatin is completely dissolved. Pour the warm mixture through a strainer into a large measuring cup with a pouring spout. Carefully pour the hot liquid into the ramekins. There will probably be a few flecks of vanilla left at the bottom of the measuring cup; spoon them over the top of

cont.

NOTE: *You can serve this in any size glass or bowl and the panna cotta will adjust accordingly. Feel free to unmold it onto a plate (but I like it best served in the glass). Instead of chocolate, try topping it with Caramel Sauce (page 32) or fruit. And if you're not a fan of finely zested orange in your sauce, try using the same amount of orange extract or 1 Tbsp of orange liqueur.*

FOOD FOR THOUGHT:
Replace "why is this happening to me?" with "what will this teach me?" (Thanks, Dad, for this one.)

each panna cotta to get some pretty flecks in the finished dish. Wrap the ramekins tightly with plastic wrap and refrigerate until set, at least 6 hours or up to overnight.

TO MAKE THE CHOCOLATE SAUCE:

1. While the panna cotta is setting up in the fridge, assemble a double boiler over low heat (or use a heatproof bowl set on top of a small pot filled with boiling water, making sure the water does not touch the bottom of the bowl). Add the chocolate, heavy cream, butter, orange zest, orange blossom water, and salt and stir until just melted. Let cool slightly and store in the fridge until ready to use. You can serve the sauce cold, at room temperature, or warmed.

TO SERVE:

1. When ready to serve, serve with chocolate sauce on the side and sprinkle with orange zest.

2. The panna cotta can be refrigerated, tightly wrapped, for up to 3 days.

Pick-Me-Up Granola

3½ cups [350 g] rolled oats

1 cup [140 g] whole-wheat flour

⅓ cup [45 g] unsalted sunflower seeds

⅓ cup [45 g] unsalted pumpkin seeds

⅓ cup [40 g] slivered almonds

1½ tsp ground cinnamon

1 tsp fine sea salt

1 cup [240 ml] maple syrup

⅔ cup [160 ml] canola oil (see Note)

1 tsp grated orange zest

1 Tbsp vanilla extract

½ cup [90 g] white chocolate chips

NOTE: *You can substitute a mild olive oil or vegetable oil for the canola oil.*

BAKING AFFIRMATION:
Something good is going to come from this. (Like that granola in the oven.)

SERVES 8

My Aunt Brenda is known for taking standard staples and turning them into art, like her excellent "pick-me-up" granola. Keep it stocked in your pantry for a delicious snack any time.

1. Preheat the oven to 350°F [180°C]. Line a baking sheet with parchment paper and coat the parchment paper with nonstick cooking spray. Set aside.

2. In a large bowl, combine the oats, flour, sunflower and pumpkin seeds, almonds, cinnamon, and salt and stir well. Set aside.

3. In a small bowl, combine the maple syrup, canola oil, orange zest, and vanilla. Pour over the dry ingredients and stir until the oats are evenly coated.

4. Pour the granola mixture onto the prepared pan and use your hands to press it into an even layer. Bake for 25 minutes, or until golden brown and fragrant. Let cool on a rack for 20 minutes.

5. While the granola cools, add the chocolate chips to a heatproof bowl. Microwave in 30-second intervals, stirring in between, until melted. When the granola is completely cool, flip the entire piece over so it's smooth-side up. Pour the melted chocolate over the granola, and spread it to the edges in a thin, even layer. Allow to cool for 15 minutes.

6. Break the granola into bite-size pieces. Store in an airtight container for up to 1 week.

You've Met Your (Banana) Matcha Loaf

BANANA BREAD

1½ cups [210 g] all-purpose flour

1 cup [200 g] sugar

2 Tbsp culinary-grade matcha powder

1 tsp baking soda

¾ tsp fine sea salt

4 large, ripe bananas

⅓ cup [80 ml] vegetable oil

¼ cup [60 ml] whole milk

¼ cup [85 g] honey

2 eggs

OPTIONAL MIX-INS

2 Tbsp chia seeds

2 Tbsp poppy seeds

⅓ cup [60 g] mini chocolate chips

FOOD FOR THOUGHT:
Sometimes it takes a bit of work, but just know that you have the power inside of you to enact the change you want—and watch it grow.

SERVES 8

There's something therapeutic about banana bread. We take brown, mushy, bananas and bake them into something delicious. It's a great metaphor for life: Regardless of what you might be going through, you have the ability to turn it into something beautiful.

1. Preheat the oven to 350°F [180°C]. Coat a 9 by 5 in [23 by 12 cm] loaf pan with butter or nonstick cooking spray and line with parchment paper, allowing the parchment to hang over the sides of the pan.

2. In a large bowl, whisk together the flour, sugar, matcha powder, baking soda, and salt.

3. In a separate large bowl, mash three of the bananas until mostly smooth with a few chunks. Add the vegetable oil, milk, honey, and eggs and stir until smooth.

4. Add the dry ingredients to the wet ingredients and stir until just combined. If you are using mix-ins, add them now. Slice the remaining banana in half lengthwise.

5. Pour the batter into the prepared pan, arranging both banana halves cut-side up on top, and bake for 60 to 65 minutes, or until a cake tester comes out clean.

6. Let cool for 10 minutes, flip onto a cooling rack, and let cool completely. Serve warm or at room temperature. The loaf will keep for 3 days at room temperature.

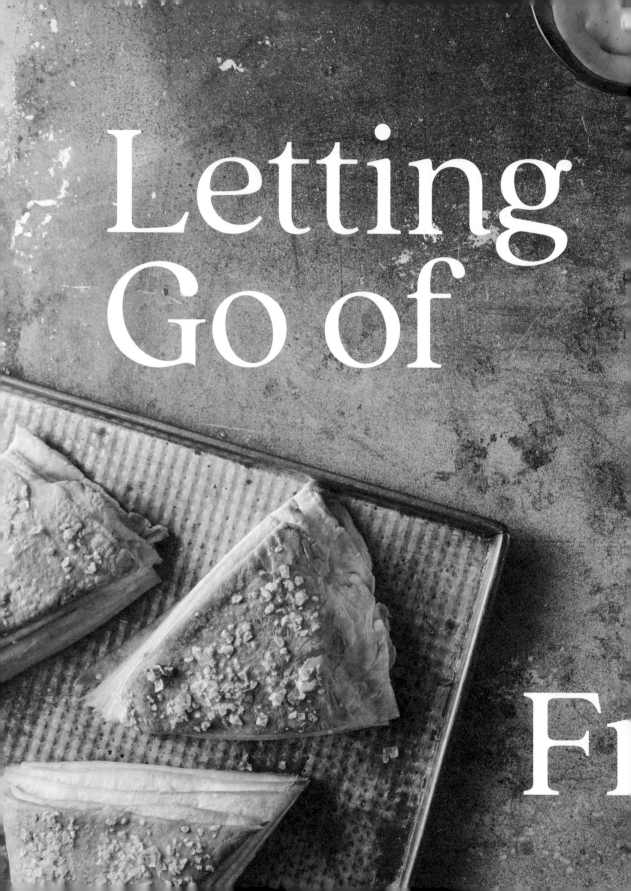

Letting
Go of
Fr

ustration

Frustration is an intense and uncomfortable feeling. People often express this feeling as anger, but behind that anger, there's usually another deeper emotion fueling the out-of-control pent-up energy.

Let's look quickly at what anger and frustration do to your body. When something happens that triggers a stress or anxious reaction, like not being heard, understood, or listened to, the body releases cortisol, a stress hormone, that puts us into a fight, flee, or freeze state. Suddenly, we're thrust into survivor mode (shout-out to Destiny's Child), and it prevents us from looking at a situation with the appropriate (rational) perspective.

Frustration is a response to all that cortisol. The mind takes that stress and anxiety and reacts with "Ugh, why is this happening?!" Stress + anxiety + frustration = a ménage à trois I've been in before that's nowhere near as fun as it sounds.

I often tell my patients that they feel so frustrated because they're out of emotional energy to take in even one more thing. The trunk is full and you just went to Costco and tried to pile it all in the back. So, what's gonna happen? That trunk isn't going to close and you're going to spill everything all over the highway, causing destruction to the other drivers. Chaos. ("It's chaos, babe," my friends are all too familiar with hearing from me. And we don't want that dark, chaotic energy, no ma'am.)

Whether the emotion that triggers the anger or frustration is disappoint-ment, sadness, or stress, the reaction is usually what people see first; it acts as a mask for how we're truly feeling. It protects us from going into how we really feel ("I don't have to explain how I really feel. I'm angry," is a phrase I hear too often from my patients). But anger isn't just an emotion. It's an energy inside of us, a fire. And as with any fire, we look to manage it so it doesn't get any bigger. Don't fan those flames! If you let it burn for too long, it will cause more damage—and that's not good for anyone.

So how do we transform these negative feelings into positive and productive actions? First, it's important to realize that frustration comes from wanting things a certain way, not getting it, and then not accepting that reality. Imagine you're stuck in a car trying to get out of a parking spot. There's a wall in front of you and a tractor trailer behind you, completely blocking you in. You try little moves to get out but you feel like you're not making any progress. It's a constant cycle of trying the same thing but expecting a different result. It's literally insanity, ya feel me? Often, you can't change the situation, but you can change your perception of it.

Even as a therapist, I am perfectly imperfect in the way I handle frustration. I would be lying if I said I hadn't caused a scene because something wasn't going my way. Cut to me on the phone with my family or sitting around the Passover seder table with them, and let me tell you, all my training on reframing my perception of frustrating situations goes right out the damn window. But instead of yelling at someone or eating something to stuff the anger and frustration away, I've learned to work through it. It all comes down to response versus reaction: Learn what triggers you, consider why it's triggering (a.k.a. the root cause of it), and then formulate your response. This three-step process allows you to work through your initially negative gut reaction so you don't spiral and say or do something you regret. In turn, there's an openness to responding in a more acceptable way.

And that's why I love spending time in the kitchen.

The quickest way to calm down and refocus is to take a deep breath. But instead of breathing exercises, let's practice some baking "yoga." Think of working in the kitchen like working out your body on a treadmill: It's a safe place to let it all out through your arms, hands, and fingers. The recipes in this chapter are intended to help you move through those feelings. Scream if you have to while kneading some dough (I've done it). Fall into the meditative rhythm of making Mint Thumbprint Cookies (page 195). As you make each indentation, take a deep breath and think or say an affirmation. Even the process of sprinkling flour onto the counter to prevent dough from sticking can be centering. You can do it lightly so it falls with grace. Or you can throw fistfuls at the counter, sending flour everywhere—even if you have to clean it up after.

If we're taking our anger out on the dough, it's not going to be directed at our interpersonal relationships. It gives us the opportunity to redirect our frustration in a way that's less destructive.

Maybe that's why I love being in the kitchen with my patients—or even by myself—because we're baking out what we're trying to say. It gives us freedom of expression. We can visualize the dough or the batter to represent the situation we're infuriated by. We're putting our thoughts and feelings into the dough, even if no one else is there to hear it. And in that moment, there isn't another side to consider. There isn't someone playing "devil's advocate" or hyping us up even further. It's just us and the dough. And dough won't talk back (unless you've had one too many glasses of chardonnay).

So, get in that kitchen and let baking help you release that energy in the most wonderful and delicious way.

Quick Session

COUNT TO 10 . . .

Take a deep breath and count to 10. Why? Because it calms us down, a lot. It lowers our blood pressure and helps us take a beat to approach a situation. While that may be a golden rule, I do have one patient I ask to count to 17; 17 seconds slows the momentum and shifts the energy caused by anger and frustration. Most of their energy is covering up what's really going on. So those extra 7 seconds gives them a bit more time to process and open up.

When it comes to recipes, we can use the time it takes to read through a recipe to start to feel our frustration leave the body. (And I don't mean scan the recipe. Actually read it! All the way through.) It refocuses our attention on something aside from what's causing the frustration. So take a deep breath, count to 10, and follow these steps to make sure your Baking Therapy doesn't become another frustration on the list.

Quick Session
. . . AND 10 TIPS TO MAKE BAKING LESS FRUSTRATING

1. **READ THE RECIPE.** Be sure to read the recipe all the way through at least once before opening that bag of flour. This will help you mentally prepare for what's ahead.

2. **MISE EN PLACE.** Portion out and put ingredients in place before starting.

3. **CHECK YOUR TEMPERATURE.** Preheat the oven and use an oven thermometer to make sure it's the right temperature.

4. **MEASURE INGREDIENTS,** and make sure you do it accurately. I prefer to weigh my baking ingredients for more precision.

5. **CHECK THE STATUS OF YOUR INGREDIENTS.** Is that water ice cold? Is that butter at room temperature?

6. **DON'T OVERMIX OR UNDERMIX.** I like to give visual cues in my recipes so you know when it's right.

7. **USE THE CORRECT TOOLS.** There's a big difference between an 8 in [20 cm] and a 9 in [23 cm] cake pan! Make sure you have the right tools at the ready before you start mixing.

8. **ALWAYS GREASE THE PAN OR LINE IT WITH PARCHMENT PAPER.** There's nothing worse than going through all that work, and the cake won't come out.

9. **LEARN WHEN TO LEAVE IT ALONE!** Don't constantly open the oven door to check on your creation; it lets heat out and keeps it from baking evenly. Things take the time they take. Don't rush it.

10. **ALLOW BAKED GOODS TO COOL.** Don't be so quick to enjoy something straight from the oven. The cooling process prevents it from falling apart and ensures the experience is frustration-free.

Churros

CINNAMON-SUGAR

¼ cup [50 g] granulated sugar

1 tsp ground cinnamon

CHURROS

2 Tbsp unsalted butter

1 Tbsp granulated sugar

1 tsp vanilla extract

½ tsp kosher salt

1 cup [140 g] all-purpose flour

1 large egg, at room temperature

Vegetable oil, for frying

DIPPING SAUCES

Chocolate hazelnut spread
(Nutella is best)

Dulce de leche (see page 176
or store-bought)

MAKES 10 CHURROS

Growing up, I spent a lot of time at the boardwalk in Deal, New Jersey, usually with a churro in hand. There's something irresistible about fried dough mixed with cinnamon and sugar. But the process of making churros can feel a little arduous. Your arms are going to get a really good workout mixing the dough. Squeezing the thick batter into batons can get frustrating. But once they hit the oil, that sizzle will bring a smile to your face.

TO MAKE THE CINNAMON-SUGAR:

1. On a small plate, mix together the sugar and cinnamon. Set aside.

TO MAKE THE CHURRO DOUGH:

1. Add 1 cup [240 ml] of water, the butter, sugar, vanilla, and salt to a 3 qt [2.8 L] saucepan and bring to a boil over medium-high heat. Once the mixture boils, add the flour all at once, turn the heat to low, and beat together with a wooden spoon or silicone spatula until the mixture has few to no lumps and a dough ball forms. Cook for 1 minute, stirring constantly, then remove from the heat and let cool for 10 minutes.

2. When the dough has cooled 140° to 160°F [60° to 70°C] on an instant-read thermometer, transfer the dough to a large mixing bowl and beat in the egg using a handheld electric mixer, stand mixer fitted with the paddle attachment, or a wooden spoon. The dough may separate at first but it will come back together.

cont.

3. Once the dough is well combined, transfer it to a pastry bag fitted with a large star-shaped tip. Alternatively, use a zip-top plastic bag with a corner snipped off. Make sure there are no air bubbles in your filled bag.

TO FRY:

1. Fill a large, heavy-bottomed pot with 1½ in [4 cm] of oil and heat it to 350°F [180°C]; check the temperature with a deep-frying thermometer. Line a plate with paper towels.

2. Either pipe 6 in [15 cm] churros directly into the oil, cutting them off as you pipe them with kitchen shears, or pipe them onto a parchment-lined baking sheet first before transferring them to the oil. Fry only two to three churros at a time, or the oil temperature will drop. Fry the churros for 6 to 7 minutes, or until golden brown all over, then remove and transfer to the prepared plate.

3. Let the churros drain briefly on the plate before tossing them in the cinnamon-sugar, making sure to coat the churros evenly. Repeat with the remaining churros, waiting for the oil to come back up to temperature before frying more.

TO BAKE:

1. Preheat the oven to 400°F [200°C]. Pipe 6 in [15 cm] churros on a parchment-lined baking sheet about 2 in [5 cm] apart and bake for 25 minutes. Turn the oven off and leave the churros in the oven for

cont.

NOTE: *If cinnamon isn't your thing, get creative! Use other spices or powdered freeze-dried fruits or replace 2 to 3 Tbsp of all-purpose flour with unsweetened cocoa powder for a hint of chocolate.*

One 14 oz [400 g] can sweetened condensed milk

4 cups [960 ml] boiling water

FOOD FOR THOUGHT:
An efficient way to work through anger is to ask yourself, "Where do I feel the anger?" After locating it, ask, "If this anger could speak, what would it say?"

10 minutes, then remove and cover with Cinnamon-Sugar Coating. If the churros feel a little dry, brush them with some melted butter before tossing with the Cinnamon-Sugar.

TO SERVE:

1. Serve warm, preferably with a rich chocolate sauce or dulce de leche for dipping.

2. These are best eaten the day they are made, although they can last up to 2 days when stored in an airtight container with a paper towel and kept at room temperature.

Dulce de Leche

1. Preheat the oven to 425°F [220°C].

2. Pour the sweetened condensed milk into an 8 in [20 cm] square pan and cover with foil. Place the pan inside a 9 by 13 in [23 by 33 cm] baking dish. Pour the boiling water into the baking dish until it reaches halfway up the smaller pan.

3. Bake until the condensed milk is dark and caramelized, about 1½ hours, adding water to the baking dish as necessary. Once darkened, remove the dulce de leche from the oven. Let it cool for 5 minutes, then whisk until smooth.

4. Serve warm or transfer it to an airtight container and put plastic wrap directly on the dulce de leche before covering. Refrigerate for up to 2 weeks.

Pecan Cinnamon Rolls

DOUGH

¾ cup [180 ml] warm whole milk, about 110°F [45°C]

2¼ tsp active dry yeast

¼ cup [50 g] plus 2 tsp granulated sugar

¼ cup [55 g] unsalted butter

1 egg plus 1 egg yolk

3 cups [420 g] bread flour

¾ tsp table salt

FILLING

⅔ cup [130 g] packed dark brown sugar

⅔ cup [80 g] pecans, roughly chopped

1½ Tbsp ground cinnamon

¼ tsp ground nutmeg

¼ cup [55 g] salted butter, at room temperature

FROSTING

4 oz [115 g] cream cheese, at room temperature

3 Tbsp unsalted butter, at room temperature

cont.

MAKES 12 ROLLS

A lot of home bakers talk about making cinnamon rolls like it's some long, terrifying process that can easily fail. Not these! I promise that you cannot get frustrated making these. Simply knead the dough, roll it out, slather on the filling, slice, and bake. I love cinnamon for its many positive effects on the brain, including increasing attention and improving memory. It can help you focus when things are getting hectic around you. Whatever is buzzing around your brain, take it out on the dough.

TO MAKE THE DOUGH:

1. In a small bowl, combine the warm milk, yeast, and 2 tsp of the granulated sugar. Set aside for 10 minutes while the yeast activates.

2. In the bowl of a stand mixer fitted with the paddle attachment, or in a large bowl using a handheld electric mixer, beat the remaining ¼ cup [50 g] of granulated sugar, the butter, egg, and egg yolk on medium speed. Add the yeast mixture and beat until combined.

3. Add the flour and salt and use a spoon or spatula to mix until the dough begins to come together. Turn out the dough onto a lightly floured surface and knead for 8 to 10 minutes. The dough should be sticky, but feel free to flour your hands if it is too sticky.

cont.

1 Tbsp maple syrup

½ tsp vanilla extract

¾ cup [90 g] powdered sugar

4. Coat a large bowl with 1 Tbsp canola oil and set the dough inside. Cover it with a damp cloth and set aside to rise for 90 minutes, or until it has doubled in size.

TO MAKE THE FILLING:

1. While the dough is proofing, in a small bowl, combine the brown sugar, pecans, cinnamon, and nutmeg.

TO ASSEMBLE AND BAKE:

1. Grease a 9 by 13 in [23 by 33 cm] baking dish.

2. Flour a work surface well and use a rolling pin to roll the dough into a rectangle a little under ½ in [13 mm] thick and 12 in [30 cm] long by 10 in [25 cm] wide. Using an offset spatula, spread the softened butter over the entire surface of the dough. Spread the filling ingredients evenly over the dough, leaving no bare edges.

3. Starting with the long side, gently roll the dough into a log and set it seam-side down. Be sure not to roll too tightly, or the cinnamon buns will bake unevenly. Slice the buns into twelve pieces about 1 in [2.5 cm] thick and nestle them cut-side up into the prepared pan (in a three-by-four bun grid). The rolls should be touching on all sides.

4. Cover the rolls with a damp cloth and set aside for 45 minutes for a second rise.

5. Preheat the oven to 350°F [180°C].

6. Bake for 20 to 30 minutes, checking frequently after the 20-minute mark to make sure they are not browning too much. The rolls are done when the center roll is just baked. If the center roll still appears raw, keep baking just a tad bit longer.

TO MAKE THE FROSTING:

1. As the rolls are baking, in the bowl of a stand mixer fitted with the paddle attachment, or in a medium bowl using a handheld electric mixer, beat the cream cheese and butter. Add the maple syrup and vanilla and beat again. Add the powdered sugar and beat until smooth.

TO SERVE:

1. When the rolls are done, allow them to cool for 10 minutes in the cake pan. Once cool enough to handle, gently transfer them to a serving dish. Spread the frosting over the cinnamon rolls and serve immediately.

BAKING AFFIRMATION:
Breathe. Redirect. Bake.

New York–Style Bagels

1½ cups [360 ml] warm
water, about 110°F [45°C]

4 tsp sugar

2 tsp active dry yeast

3½ cups [490 g] bread flour

2 tsp fine kosher salt

1 egg

TOPPINGS

Everything bagel seasoning,
sesame seeds, cinnamon sugar,
Asiago cheese—whatever
your heart desires, babe!

MAKES 8 BAGELS

Ask any New Yorker and they'll tell you about their
favorite bagel—and then argue about why it's better than
yours (I wish I were kidding). So, as a Jewish New Yorker,
bagels are near and dear to me. If you're lucky enough to
live in New York, you probably have access to fresh bagels
every morning. But if you live outside this wonderful city,
or even just want to give your wallet a break from the
neighborhood bakery, you need to try these fresh bagels.
They are infinitely tastier than the ones you buy at the
supermarket. There's nothing better than a warm, fresh-
from-the-oven bagel, so I recommend eating these as soon
as they're done!

1. Line a baking sheet with parchment paper.

2. In a small bowl, combine the warm water, sugar,
    and yeast. Set aside for 10 minutes while the
    yeast activates.

3. In a large bowl, combine the flour and salt. Add the
    yeast mixture and use a wooden spoon to stir until
    the dough comes together enough to knead with
    your hands. If the dough won't absorb all the flour
    after a few minutes of kneading, add more water,
    1 Tbsp at a time. Knead the dough by hand until it
    becomes firm and smooth, 5 to 7 minutes.

4. Divide the kneaded dough into eight equal portions
    and form each piece into a ball. Place the dough
    balls on the prepared baking sheet. Cover with a

damp cloth and allow to rise for about 1 hour, or until doubled in size.

5. Use your finger to punch a hole into the center of each dough ball, then use your fingers to work the hole into a circle about 2 in [5 cm] wide. Re-cover the dough and allow it to rest for another 10 minutes.

6. Preheat the oven to 425°F [220°C]. Fill a large stock-pot with water and bring to a boil.

7. Use a large slotted spoon to lower each bagel into the boiling water, making sure not to overcrowd them. Allow the bagels to boil for 2 minutes on each side, then shake off the excess water and place them back on the baking sheet.

8. In a small bowl, whip the egg and 1 Tbsp of water together until incorporated. Using a pastry brush, brush the tops of the bagels with the beaten egg. If you are using a topping, sprinkle it over the bagels. Bake for 25 minutes, or until the bagels turn a light golden color. Let cool for 5 minutes before serving.

9. These are best eaten fresh but will keep in an airtight container for 3 or 4 days.

FOOD FOR THOUGHT:
Many people don't know that frustration, as a feeling, takes only 90 seconds to pass if you choose not to dwell on it. So, practice reaching for a different emotion while you make this recipe. Try a breathing exercise where you breathe in for 4 seconds, hold for just a moment, then breathe out for 8 seconds. Repeat this pattern until the dough has risen, and you will have achieved a better state of mind.

Bakery-Style Cinnamon Swirl Bread with Raisins

BREAD

⅓ cup [80 ml] warm water, about 110°F [45°C]

Two ¼ oz [7 g] packages active dry yeast

5½ cups [770 g] all-purpose flour

1 cup [240 ml] warm whole milk, about 110°F [45°C]

1 cup [200 g] sugar

2 eggs, at room temperature

6 Tbsp [90 g] unsalted butter, at room temperature

1½ tsp fine sea salt

2 Tbsp ground cinnamon

Pinch of ground cardamom

1 cup [140 g] raisins

TOPPING

3 Tbsp unsalted butter, melted

3 Tbsp sugar

1 tsp ground cinnamon

MAKES 2 LOAVES

Do you remember when you were a kid and waking up to freshly toasted and buttered cinnamon swirl bread from Pepperidge Farms? Wasn't it the best? It's kind of cheating for breakfast. Seriously, sweet bread? How did our parents fall for it? This recipe is a nod to that childhood breakfast treat. Baking bread teaches patience, which is the antidote to frustration. The better you are at practicing patience—kneading the dough, waiting for it to rise, and then waiting for it to bake—the better you will be able to handle frustration.

TO MAKE THE BREAD:

1. Grease two 9 by 5 in [23 by 12 cm] loaf pans with butter or nonstick cooking spray, line with parchment paper, and set aside.

2. In the bowl of a stand mixer fitted with the paddle attachment, combine the warm water and yeast. Set aside for 10 minutes while the yeast activates.

3. Add 2¾ cups [385 g] of the flour, the warm milk, ½ cup [100 g] of the sugar, the eggs, butter, and salt to the yeast mixture. Mix on low speed to combine, then on medium speed for a few minutes, or until the dough is smooth. Add the remaining 2¾ cups [385 g] of flour and mix again on medium speed.

4. Turn out the dough onto a floured surface and knead for 5 to 7 minutes, or until smooth. Grease a large bowl, place the dough inside, flip over the

dough to grease the top, cover with a clean dish towel, and let rise in a warm spot for about 1 hour, or until doubled in size.

5. In a small bowl, mix the cinnamon and cardamom with the remaining ½ cup [100 g] of sugar and set aside.

6. Turn out the dough onto a lightly floured surface and divide in half. Roll each half into a rectangle about 18 by 8 in [46 by 20 cm]. Sprinkle each one with half of the cinnamon-sugar mixture. Sprinkle on the raisins and press them in slightly with your palm so they stick. Roll up (starting with the short side) and place each loaf, seam-side down, in the prepared loaf pans.

7. Cover with the dish towel and let rise in a warm spot until doubled in size, about 90 minutes.

8. Preheat the oven to 350°F [180°C].

9. Bake the loaves on the middle rack of the oven for 30 to 35 minutes, until firm and nicely browned.

TO MAKE THE TOPPING AND SERVE:

1. Just before the loaves are done, in a small mixing bowl, combine the melted butter, sugar, and cinnamon until combined.

2. Spread the topping over the loaves immediately once they come out of the oven. Let cool completely before slicing. Store leftovers in the fridge for up to 3 days.

BAKING AFFIRMATION:
Today I choose to respond rather than react.

Jack's Chocolate Chip Cookies

2 cups [280 g] all-purpose flour

1 cup [120 g] cake flour

1½ tsp kosher salt

1 tsp baking powder

1 tsp baking soda

1 cup [220 g] unsalted butter, cut into small chunks

1 cup [200 g] granulated sugar

1 cup [200 g] packed light brown sugar

2 tsp vanilla extract

1 egg plus 2 egg yolks

1¼ cup [225 g] mix of chopped semisweet, dark, and white chocolate

Flaky sea salt, for topping

Chocolate Ganache (page 30), heated until runny (optional)

MAKES 45 COOKIES

Who hasn't had an awful day saved by a chocolate chip cookie? Some jerk yelled at you on the subway? You stepped in gum and didn't notice until it stuck to your favorite expensive rug? You missed that super-important phone call you'd been waiting on all day? A good chocolate chip cookie can make you feel better, but a great chocolate chip cookie can really save the day. These cookies are so good not only because of their decadence, but also because they are visually pleasing, thanks to three different types of chocolate to add texture and beauty. Let it all out on these cookies. You have to chop and crush the chips, so do it with gusto!

1. Preheat the oven to 350°F [180°C]. Line two baking sheets with parchment paper and set aside.

2. In a large bowl, stir together the all-purpose flour, cake flour, kosher salt, baking powder, and baking soda and set aside.

3. In the bowl of a stand mixer fitted with the paddle attachment, or in a medium bowl using a handheld electric mixer, beat the butter, granulated sugar, and brown sugar on medium speed until combined. Add the vanilla and beat again, then add the egg and egg yolks one at a time, beating after each addition. Turn the mixer to low speed and add the dry ingredients. Then, add ¼ cup [45 g] of the chocolate and mix until just combined.

cont.

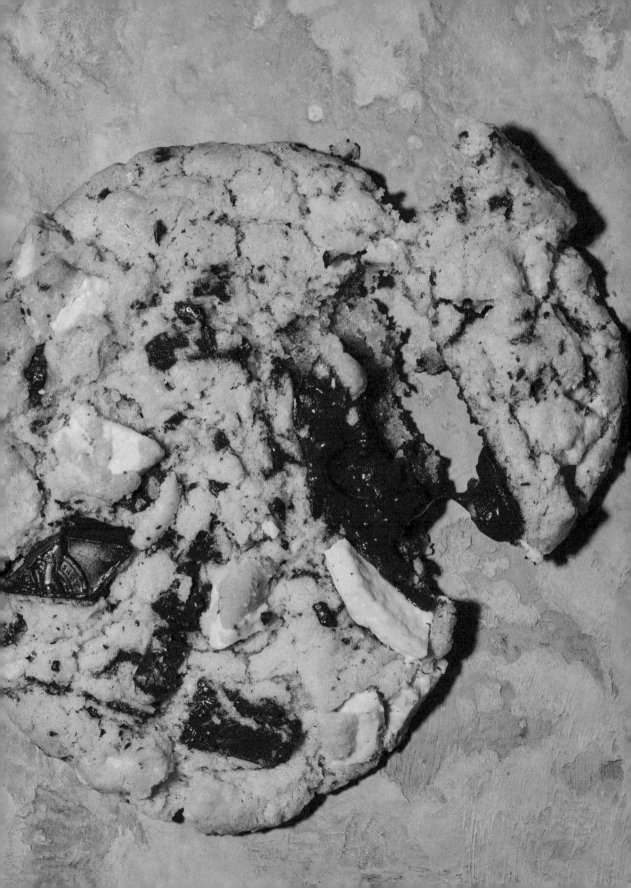

4. Using a medium cookie scoop, scoop balls of dough onto the prepared baking sheets, 2 in [5 cm] apart. Top each ball with a piece of the remaining chocolate. Press lightly into the top of the dough.

5. Bake for 12 to 13 minutes, or until the bottoms just begin to brown. Immediately sprinkle with the flaky sea salt and let cool for 15 minutes on the baking sheet before cooling completely on a cooling rack.

6. Once the cookies are cooled, dip them halfway into the ganache, if desired, and place them back onto the cooling rack for the ganache to harden. Store leftovers in the fridge for up to 5 days.

FOOD FOR THOUGHT:
You have only so much energy to give. You can't tend to the other areas in your life if you're always revved up. Don't waste it all on frustration and anger.

Soft Pretzel Triangles

1 cup warm water [240 ml], about 110°F [45°C]

2 tsp active dry yeast

2 tsp sugar

4 cups [560 g] all-purpose flour

1 tsp sea salt (for savory)

Cinnamon-Sugar (for sweet) (page 173)

7 Tbsp [105 g] salted butter, at room temperature

¼ cup [45 g] baking soda

Coarse salt (for savory)

MAKES 8 PRETZELS

A warm, fresh soft pretzel can be so soothing. When the people in your life are stressing you out and you're sick of everyone's garbage, whip up a batch of these pretzels for an at-home movie night. Sit down with your fresh-baked yummy treats and shut out the world. Serve these with butter, mustard, honey, cheese sauce, or whatever your heart desires. With the kneading and stacking, these pretzels give you an opportunity to physically release your feelings through your hands.

1. In a small bowl, combine the warm water, yeast, and sugar. Set aside for 10 minutes while the yeast activates.

2. Meanwhile, in a large bowl, whisk together the flour and either the sea salt or 1 Tbsp of the cinnamon-sugar (depending on whether you want sweet or savory pretzels). Add the yeast mixture and 1 Tbsp of butter and use a wooden spoon to mix the ingredients until the mixture comes together enough for you to knead it with your hands.

3. Knead the dough in the bowl until it is smooth and elastic, 5 to 8 minutes. Pour 1 Tbsp olive oil into a clean large bowl and swirl it around to coat the bowl. Place the dough in the bowl and cover it with a dish towel. Set aside to rise in a warm place for 1 hour.

4. Punch down the dough and knead it in the bowl for 5 more minutes. On your work surface, gather the dough into a ball and cut it into six equal pieces.

cont.

5. Use a rolling pin to roll each piece of dough into a 10 to 12 in [25 to 30.5 cm] round. Butter the top of each round with 1 Tbsp of the remaining butter and stack the rounds like pancakes. Set the dough in the fridge to chill for 30 minutes.

6. While the dough chills, add 6 cups [1.4 L] water and the baking soda to a deep skillet (deep enough to submerge the pretzels). Bring to a simmer.

7. Preheat the oven to 400°F [200°C]. Line a plate with paper towels and set aside.

8. Remove the dough from the fridge and, using a sharp knife, cut the stack into 8 equal wedges, as if you were cutting a pie. Using a slotted spoon, quickly dip each stacked wedge into the simmering water for around 20 seconds. Drain the wedges on the paper towels. If they begin to fall apart, don't worry. Just restack them!

9. Line a baking sheet with parchment paper and place each dough wedge onto the baking sheet. Depending on whether you are making the pretzels savory or sweet, sprinkle the tops with coarse salt or some of the remaining cinnamon-sugar (you may not use it all).

10. Bake for 20 to 25 minutes, or until the pretzels are golden brown on top and around the edges. Serve warm. To store, allow the pretzels to cool completely and keep in an airtight container at room temperature for up to 3 days.

BAKING AFFIRMATION:
Feelings aren't facts. I can express my frustration and remain in control.

Soft and Flaky Biscuits

1 cup [220 g] frozen unsalted butter, plus 1 Tbsp melted butter, for brushing

2¼ cup [315 g] all-purpose flour

½ tsp sugar

4 tsp baking powder

1½ tsp kosher salt

¼ tsp freshly ground black pepper (optional)

¾ cup [180 g] Greek yogurt

½ cup [120 ml] whole milk

Flaky sea salt, for sprinkling

MAKES 6 BISCUITS

One of my favorite childhood memories is visiting Delicious Apple Orchards in New Jersey with my family. They made fresh biscuits on-site, right in front of your eyes. I could smell the butter as soon as we set foot on the property, and it could make even the worst day better. Try to release a little of your frustration with each biscuit you cut. Then, when you gather those final scraps, make a conscious effort to release your feelings with the very last biscuit.

1. Using the large holes of a box grater, grate the frozen butter into a small bowl. Put the bowl in the freezer to refreeze the butter for at least 30 minutes.

2. In a large bowl, whisk the flour, sugar, baking powder, salt, and pepper (if using). Set the bowl aside in the freezer with the butter.

3. Preheat the oven to 425°F [220°C]. Line a baking sheet with parchment paper.

4. In a small bowl, whisk together the Greek yogurt and milk until smooth. Set aside. Add the frozen grated butter to the dry ingredients and mix quickly with your fingers. Once the butter pieces are covered in flour, add the yogurt mixture and mix gently with your hands or a large spoon. The dough will look shaggy—do not add more liquid.

NOTE: *You can easily double this recipe and freeze the cut biscuit dough. If you bake them from frozen, add 2 to 3 minutes to the total baking time. The key to this recipe is temperature: frozen butter with cold dry ingredients in a cold bowl. Be gentle and don't overwork the dough, which leads to a tough biscuit. Push straight down and up when cutting biscuits with a biscuit cutter. Don't twist or spin the cutter.*

5. Flip the dough onto a lightly floured work surface and push it together with your hands to form a large mound. Roll it out with a rolling pin into a 12 by 8 in [30.5 by 20 cm] rectangle. Fold the dough lengthwise into thirds in the shape of a business letter, so you end up with three layers of dough. Repeat the rolling and folding process for a total of four times. Roll the dough into an 8 by 6 in [20 by 15 cm] rectangle that is 1 in [2.5 cm] thick, trimming the edges with a floured knife to prevent sticking. Use a knife to cut the dough into eight equal rectangles and place on the prepared baking sheet.

6. Brush the biscuits with melted butter, sprinkle with sea salt, and bake for 18 to 20 minutes, or until golden brown.

7. Serve immediately.

Cheesecake with a Pomegranate Twist

POMEGRANATE SAUCE

2 cups [480 ml] pomegranate juice

½ cup [100 g] sugar

3 Tbsp cornstarch

CRUST

2½ cups [300 g] graham cracker crumbs

½ cup [110 g] unsalted butter, melted

2 Tbsp sugar

FILLING

6 eggs, separated

1¼ cups [250 g] sugar

¼ cup [60 ml] fresh lemon juice

1 Tbsp grated lemon zest

1½ tsp vanilla extract

1½ lb [680 g] cream cheese, cut into small chunks

½ cup [70 g] all-purpose flour

1 cup [240 ml] heavy cream

SERVES 12

This cheesecake reinvents a very overdone dessert. It's unique, has a tall and stunning crust, and an antioxidant-filled injection of color from the pomegranate. Feeding your body antioxidants gives it the boost it needs to deal with stress, and the soul boost you'll get from this cake's sweet, luscious flavor will brighten your day!

TO MAKE THE POMEGRANATE SAUCE:

1. In a saucepan over medium-high heat, combine the pomegranate juice, sugar, and cornstarch and heat until it bubbles and thickens. Cook, stirring, until the liquid is reduced to 1½ cups [360 ml], about 5 minutes. Let the sauce come to room temperature and then set aside in the fridge to chill.

TO MAKE THE CRUST:

1. In a medium bowl, combine the graham cracker crumbs, melted butter, and sugar. Press the mixture into a 9 in [23 cm] springform pan, using a glass or your hands to press it into the bottom and up the sides of the pan. It doesn't matter whether the crust goes entirely up the sides. Refrigerate for 30 minutes. After 30 minutes, wrap the bottom of the springform pan in aluminum foil so it almost comes up to the top.

2. Preheat the oven to 350°F [180°C].

cont.

TO MAKE THE FILLING:

1. In the bowl of a stand mixer fitted with the paddle attachment, or in a medium bowl using a handheld electric mixer, beat the egg yolks, sugar, lemon juice, lemon zest, and vanilla on medium speed. Add the cream cheese a few small chunks at a time and beat until combined. Add the flour and beat on medium-high speed for 7 to 8 minutes, until smooth.

2. In a separate bowl, beat the egg whites until they form soft peaks. In a third bowl, whip the heavy cream until it forms soft peaks. Using a rubber spatula, fold the egg whites and whipped cream into the egg yolk mixture.

TO ASSEMBLE AND BAKE:

1. Scrape the filling into the pan on top of the crust and tent aluminum foil over the top. Set the foil-wrapped springform pan in a 12 in [30.5 cm] round ovenproof skillet or pan and place both on the middle rack of the oven. Fill the larger pan with water that reaches halfway up the side of the springform pan. Bake for about 2 hours, or until the edges of the cake set but the middle still jiggles. Remove the aluminum foil for the last 10 to 15 minutes for a little bit of color. The top might crack or rise and then sink—that is OK. The pomegranate sauce will cover all issues.

2. Remove from the oven and let cool to room temperature on a cooling rack, then refrigerate for at least 4 hours before serving. Drizzle the pomegranate sauce on the whole cheesecake or on individual slices before serving.

BAKING AFFIRMATION:
Today I allow myself to fully feel my frustration at my own pace.

Mint Thumbprint Cookies

COOKIES

4 oz [115 g] bittersweet chocolate, finely chopped

1½ cups [210 g] all-purpose flour

½ cup [40 g] unsweetened cocoa powder

¾ tsp fine sea salt

1 cup [220 g] unsalted butter, at room temperature

⅓ cup [65 g] granulated sugar

2 Tbsp packed light brown sugar

2 egg yolks

1 tsp vanilla extract

½ cup [100 g] Swedish pearl sugar (you can replace with either ½ cup [115 g] sanding sugar or ½ cup [70 g] finely chopped nuts)

FILLING

6 oz [170 g] white chocolate, finely chopped

¼ cup plus 2 Tbsp [90 ml] heavy cream

½ tsp peppermint extract

1 or 2 drops of green food coloring (optional)

½ cup [90 g] Junior Mints candies, chopped (optional)

MAKES 40 COOKIES

These yummy little bites allow you to please your palate and your mind at the same time. Why? Because mint is a soothing aromatic that has a cooling effect on the body. Mint also naturally boosts your mood and increases your mind's ability to process information. Talk about an excellent antidote to the midday slumps. And the process of pushing your thumb into each cookie helps you release the tension, one indent at a time.

TO MAKE THE COOKIES:

1. In a microwave-safe bowl, heat the bittersweet chocolate in 20-second increments until melted and smooth. Stir and set aside to cool.

2. In a medium bowl, combine the flour, cocoa powder, and salt.

3. In the bowl of a stand mixer fitted with the paddle attachment, or in a medium bowl using a handheld electric mixer, beat the butter, granulated sugar, and brown sugar on medium speed until creamy and smooth. Add the egg yolks, vanilla, and cooled chocolate mixture and beat to combine. Turn the mixer to low, add the dry ingredients, and beat until just incorporated. Place the dough in a bowl, tightly wrap with plastic wrap, and refrigerate for at least 1 hour.

4. Preheat the oven to 350°F [180°C]. Line two baking sheets with parchment paper.

cont.

5. Using a small cookie scoop, scoop out 1 Tbsp of dough and roll into balls.

6. Put the Swedish pearl sugar in a shallow bowl and roll the dough balls in the sugar to coat. Place on the prepared baking sheets. Using your thumb or the bottom of a wine cork, make an indentation in the middle of each cookie. Don't go all the way through to the baking sheet, just halfway. Bake for 10 minutes, use the wine cork or another heat-safe tool to remake the indents in the cookies, and bake for an additional 5 minutes. Let cool completely.

TO MAKE THE FILLING:

1. Place the white chocolate in a small bowl and set aside.

2. Heat the heavy cream in a microwave-safe bowl until boiling (about 20-second bursts) and pour over the white chocolate. Stir in the peppermint extract and green food coloring (if using).

TO ASSEMBLE:

1. Fill the thumbprints with the mint filling and top with some chopped Junior Mints, if desired. Refrigerate for at least 30 minutes, or until fully set. Store leftovers in the fridge for up to 3 days.

FOOD FOR THOUGHT:
Just because one area in your life isn't working out the way you want it to doesn't mean everything else is like that. Try to focus on what's right rather than what's wrong.

Slap-It-Together Focaccia

2 cups [480 ml] warm water, about 110°F [45°C]

2 tsp active dry yeast

1 tsp sugar

4½ cups [630 g] all-purpose flour

2 tsp fine salt

4 Tbsp [60 ml] olive oil

2 tsp flaky sea salt, for sprinkling

2 to 3 Tbsp chopped fresh rosemary

MAKES 12 PIECES

On a family trip to Italy for my mother's birthday (don't worry, Mom, I won't say which one), we ended up taking a cooking class from an Italian grandmother on the outskirts of Puglia, Italy, and that is where I learned to make this focaccia. Focaccia actually requires a few good slaps to make it perfect—who knew!—which is a great opportunity to work out some of those overwhelming feelings.

1. In the bowl of a stand mixer fitted with the dough hook attachment, combine the water, yeast, and sugar. Set aside for 5 minutes while the yeast activates.

2. Add the flour and salt to the yeast mixture and mix on low speed, until all the flour is absorbed by the water and a very loose, sticky dough forms, 3 to 4 minutes. Continue to mix, either in the stand mixer or by hand with a wooden spoon, for about 1 minute. Cover the bowl with plastic wrap and let sit in a warm spot for 2 hours, until the dough mass rises and has lots of sponge bubbles on the top.

3. Coat a 9 by 13 in [23 by 33 cm] metal baking dish with 2 Tbsp of oil. Scoop the dough out of the bowl and into the pan, scraping all the bits of dough that stick to the bowl. Oil your fingers to prevent sticking, and press the dough out to the edges and corners. If the dough retracts a bit, that's OK. Cover with plastic wrap and let sit in a warm spot for 1 hour.

NOTE: *This recipe is very flexible. Here are some swaps if you want to experiment: Add ⅔ cup [about 50 g] of your favorite shredded cheese to the dough once it has been mixed; replace the rosemary with a clove of minced garlic, fresh tarragon, or sage for a different scent profile.*

4. Preheat the oven to 450°F [230°C].

5. Remove the plastic wrap and drizzle the remaining 2 Tbsp of oil over the dough. Gently spread all over the surface of the dough with your fingers to coat the top. Then using your fingertips in a claw motion, push down until they reach the pan's bottom, creating dimples in the dough all over. Little bubbles may start to appear. Top with sea salt and fresh rosemary.

6. Bake for 30 to 35 minutes, or until the dough is golden brown.

7. Cut into slices and serve warm or at room temperature. Store leftovers in the fridge for up to 2 days.

FOOD FOR THOUGHT:
This is one of the few times in life that you are allowed to slap something and it's totally fine. If you're feeling frustrated, bake this focaccia and slap it out!

Connecti
with Othe

Human beings are social animals, and we're wired to relate to others. (Relationship = *how* we do that.) Seeking a sense of connection with others is a natural desire, and the lack of relational connection is often at the root of many things I work through with my patients. The quality of our relationships is marked by how bonded we are to other people. The strength of our relationships, or the lack thereof, impacts our mental health and well-being.

So, how do you connect? In order to answer that, we must first look at the elements of what make up an authentic connection rather than a superficial one. A relationship that's not based in authenticity is like having Splenda when your body really wants sugar. It's still sweet, but it's not going to really satisfy you in the same way.

Think about your friends. Who are the ones you would call when you're in trouble? An intimate friend, one that's part of your inner circle (the ride-or-die type of friend), right? You probably don't have dozens of intimate friends; it's an honor reserved for the best of the best.

Authentic relationships are set apart from acquaintanceships by both shared experiences and shared empathy. You form connections with people who have things in common with you. You create a bond when you feel like you can relate to their experiences (without making it all about you). But what really takes the relationship to the next level is shared empathy. Empathy moves beyond shared experiences and into shared feelings. It's about finding that right balance in the relationship, whether it's a friend, family member, or significant other. The same goes for baking; finding the right balance of ingredients is going to determine how the final product comes out of the oven.

I enjoy whenever my patients ask for the CliffsNotes version of how to connect with someone. As with baking, there are unfortunately no short-cuts to take—you just have to put in the work.

Real connection can feel scary! Because it's so rare, we're not used to it. It's hard to take the first step in communicating because it's uncomfort-able to start, even if, or especially if, you're trying to deepen a relationship with someone who is already important to you. Those situations tend to shut us down.

But you know what is a stellar conversation starter? Food! Think about it: Life happens in the kitchen. Our fondest memories are often created here, and it is a gathering place for the people we care about. Food helps break the ice. It's about (baking and) breaking bread.

When you bake with someone, you're automatically opening up the lines of communication. Why? Because following a recipe requires a dialogue: dividing up the responsibilities, talking through each step. You can't bake together if you can't talk to each other; the fate of the final product depends on your teamwork and communication (make a note of that). This is something my Grandma Raquel instilled in me when I joined her in the kitchen to make Guatemalan treats to share with our family. When you finally get that dough in the oven, you have time to sit and talk to each other. So, make the most of it!

My grandmother first introduced me to the power of connecting with others through baking. I never found myself to be "one of the boys" in school—I never felt like I could connect with my peers over things like basketball (or any sport, for that matter). On Thursdays, I would run to my grandma's house to bake challah with her. That was my safe space.

As we made the challah each week, she took an interest in me. We talked about her and her upbringing in the Syrian Jewish community in Brooklyn. We weren't just connecting as grandma and grandson. We were connecting through our heritage as well. Those Thursday afternoons taught me so much (and I miss her dearly).

One of the best parts of those Thursdays was that we didn't keep the finished product to ourselves; it would become the centerpiece of the big family Shabbat dinner on Friday. It extended the connection that my grandma and I shared to the rest of the family. I like to call this "community through carbs." As we broke bread to start Shabbat, we were not only sharing something delicious, but we were also uniting over our history, our days, and with lots of laughs along the way.

That's what makes Baking Therapy so powerful. These recipes are meant to be either baked together or shared with others. You can do both. Either way, it's about sharing! Invite someone over to help make some Cookies and Cream Brownies (page 225). Or maybe they'll love the gorgeous texture and flavor of I Crumble for You Coffee Cake (page 211)—bake and bring them some!

So, what are you waiting for? Grab your spouse, your best friend, your neighbor, the kids. Or just go at it solo. Bust out the baking sheets and the Tupperware. It's time to connect!

Quick Session
CREATING INTIMACY

Sustaining intimacy in relationships, whether romantic or not, is often difficult. Once you stop feeling seen and appreciated by your loved one, you often stop feeling comfortable or confident enough to let each other in and then end up drifting apart.

But creating intimacy isn't as grueling as it sounds. It's a bit like baking. Baking requires an understanding of what will make a recipe really sing or what causes it to fail. The same goes for relationships. If you're able to communicate with each other about what pushes your buttons, what makes you happy or sad, then you'll be able to develop a strong, intimate bond with each other.

Instead of "intimacy," I like to call this practice "into-me-see": an invitation that allows for someone to see your vulnerable side. Real intimacy is based on trust and understanding, so don't be afraid to let down the drawbridge to the guarded palace of your life. To do that, head into the kitchen.

As simple as it sounds, doing things together that require collaboration, like baking, will get you back into the practice of connecting. You're looking for ways to close the space between you. And what better way to do that than with a deliciously sweet or savory treat!

Early on in relationships, you express curiosity about one another. You find common interests and become a safe space for each other. However, as years go by, you might find you have precious little in common at all. (Insert that awkward silence here.)

But it's important to remember that you're allowed to like different things from time to time. It just means you might need to put in a bit more effort. (Both of you should.) Remember, you get out of the kitchen what you put into it. The same goes for your relationship.

Lemon Ricotta Fritters

1 cup [140 g] all-purpose flour

¼ cup [50 g] granulated sugar

2 tsp baking powder

½ tsp ground coriander

Grated zest of 1 large lemon

1 cup [240 g] ricotta cheese

3 eggs, at room temperature

1 tsp lemon extract

½ tsp vanilla extract

6 cups [1.4 L] vegetable oil

Powdered sugar, for topping

Honey, for topping

FOOD FOR THOUGHT:
Good conversations happen
over food. Great conversations
happen over baked goods.

SERVES 8

I love—like really love—a good lemon ricotta pancake for breakfast. But if you're in the mood for something a little more special, try these fritters instead! They're bite-size, battered, and deep-fried, so it'll feel like you're having dessert for breakfast. Yum!

1. In a large bowl, whisk together the flour, granulated sugar, baking powder, coriander, and lemon zest.

2. In a separate small bowl, whisk together the ricotta, eggs, lemon extract, and vanilla until smooth, then pour over the flour mixture. Whisk until the mixture is well combined and no lumps remain. Set aside.

3. In a wide Dutch oven or deep skillet, heat the oil over medium-high heat. You want to shoot for around 350°F [180°C], or if you don't have a thermometer, you can test with a tiny piece of the dough. If it sizzles, the oil is warm enough. If the oil is too cold or too hot, the dough will either sink or burn too quickly, respectively. Line a plate with paper towels.

4. Carefully drop the batter into the oil by heaping teaspoonfuls, being sure not to overcrowd them. Fry in batches for 3 to 4 minutes each, occasionally flipping the fritters in the oil so that both sides brown evenly.

5. Remove the fritters from the oil and drain on the prepared plate.

6. Sprinkle the cooked fritters with powdered sugar and then drizzle with honey. Serve immediately.

Tropical Fruit Tart

CRUST

1 cup [140 g] all-purpose flour

½ cup [55 g] sweetened coconut flakes

½ tsp fine sea salt

½ cup [110 g] cold unsalted butter, cubed

1 large egg, separated

¼ tsp coconut extract

TOPPING

1 cup [240 ml] cold heavy cream

8 oz [230 g] mascarpone, at room temperature

¼ cup [30 g] powdered sugar

1 tsp vanilla extract

1 large mango, peeled, pitted, and sliced

2 kiwis, peeled and sliced

Honey, for drizzling (optional)

SERVES 8

I love a good summer barbecue, if only for the desserts like a fruit tart. This version is a little more elevated but just as fuss-free. This recipe is also kid-friendly: When it comes time to add the fruit toppings, ask them to help. The key: Have fun and be creative!

TO MAKE THE CRUST:

1. In a food processor, process the flour, coconut flakes, and salt until the coconut is finely chopped. Add the butter and pulse until the butter is in pea-size pieces and fine crumbs form. If making by hand, finely chop the coconut flakes and mix it with the flour and salt before rubbing the butter in with your fingers until the mixture has the consistency of coarse bread crumbs.

2. In a small bowl, mix the egg yolk and coconut extract with 2 Tbsp of cold water and add it to the flour mixture. Pulse the food processor until a dough forms, or if making by hand, just knead the dough until it comes together in a ball. Wrap the tart dough in plastic wrap and refrigerate for at least 1 hour or up to overnight.

3. Unwrap the tart dough and roll it out on a floured work surface to ⅛ inch [3 mm] thick. Gently fit the dough into a 9 in [23 cm] round tart pan with a removable bottom. Trim the excess dough from the edges. Place the pan in the fridge for 30 minutes to chill.

4. Preheat the oven to 350°F [180°C].

5. Remove the pan from the fridge and place parchment paper in the middle of the crust. Fill with pie weights, such as dried beans or uncooked rice, and bake for 20 minutes, or until the edges of the crust are golden. Remove the parchment paper and weights before brushing the crust all over with the remaining egg white. Bake for another 10 to 15 minutes, or until the bottom of the pie is golden brown and dry. Remove and let cool completely before topping.

TO MAKE THE TOPPING AND SERVE:

1. In a large bowl of a stand mixer fitted with the whisk attachment or with a handheld electric mixer, whisk the heavy cream until stiff peaks form. Set aside.

2. In another large bowl with a stand mixer fitted with the paddle attachment or using a handheld electric mixer, beat the mascarpone, powdered sugar, and vanilla on medium speed until combined and fluffy.

3. Add one-fourth of the whipped cream to the mascarpone mixture and fold with a silicone spatula. Once loosened, add the rest of the whipped cream to the mascarpone mixture and fold gently until combined. Add the mixture to the cooled tart crust and refrigerate for at least 4 hours or overnight.

4. Top the tart with sliced mango, kiwi, and a drizzle of honey, if desired. Gently remove the tart from the pan and serve. Store leftovers in the fridge for up to 2 days.

FOOD FOR THOUGHT:
Before you start preparing a dish, set an intention for how you'll share the finished product—and with who.

I Crumble for You Coffee Cake

CRUMB

½ cup [110 g] salted butter, melted

⅓ cup [65 g] granulated sugar

⅓ cup [65 g] packed dark brown sugar

2 tsp ground cinnamon

1 tsp ground nutmeg

Pinch of salt

1½ cups [180 g] cake flour

CAKE

⅓ cup [80 ml] whole milk

1 tsp fresh lemon juice

1¼ cups [150 g] cake flour, sifted

1½ tsp ground cinnamon

1 tsp baking powder

½ tsp table salt

¼ tsp baking soda

6 Tbsp [90 g] unsalted butter, at room temperature

½ cup [100 g] granulated sugar

1 egg

½ cup [120 g] sour cream

cont.

SERVES 9

I'll say it again in case it wasn't clear: I love a good crumb! My obsession started when I was little. My grandma Raquel always had Entenmann's coffee cakes around the pool—much to my grandfather's delight. We would sit down together, talk about our lives, and share these little cakes (sometimes she'd let me have more if I didn't tell my mom). We would connect over the crumb, and connection is really the best gift you can give someone.

1. Preheat the oven to 325°F [170°C]. (This will prevent the cake from browning too much during its long cooking time.) Coat a 8 in [20 cm] square baking dish with nonstick cooking spray and set aside.

TO MAKE THE CRUMB:

1. In a large bowl, whisk together the butter, granulated sugar, brown sugar, cinnamon, nutmeg, and salt. Slowly add the flour and mix with a wooden spoon until everything is incorporated. Use your hands to form the mixture into a flat disk and wrap it in plastic wrap. Set aside.

TO MAKE THE CAKE:

1. In a small bowl, combine the milk and lemon juice. Set aside for 5 minutes to curdle.

2. In a large bowl, whisk together the flour, cinnamon, baking powder, salt, and baking soda.

cont.

1½ Tbsp vanilla extract

¼ cup [30 g] chopped pecans (optional)

3. In the bowl of a stand mixer fitted with the paddle attachment, or in a medium bowl using a handheld electric mixer, beat the butter and sugar on low speed until fluffy. Add the egg, sour cream, vanilla, and milk mixture and beat on medium speed for 2 minutes, beating after each addition and scraping down the bowl as needed. Add the dry ingredients and beat until incorporated.

4. Pour the cake batter into the prepared pan and level it with an offset spatula. Unwrap the crumble mixture and break it into pieces over the cake batter. If using the chopped pecans, break half of the crumble pieces over the top, add 2 Tbsp of pecans, then add the other half of the crumble and top with the remaining 2 Tbsp of pecans. Try to leave some larger pieces of the crumble in the mix.

5. Bake for 40 to 45 minutes, or until a fork stuck in the center comes out clean. Let cool for 30 minutes to 1 hour, slice into squares, and serve. Store leftovers in an airtight container for up to 4 days at room temperature.

BAKING AFFIRMATION:
In the kitchen, I'm able to share more than good food. I can share parts of myself too.

Jumpin' Java Cake

CAKE

⅓ cup [25 g] unsweetened cocoa powder, plus more for dusting

1¼ cups [175 g] all-purpose flour

1 cup [200 g] sugar

1 tsp baking soda

½ tsp table salt

1 cup [240 ml] warm, strong black coffee

⅓ cup [80 g] coconut oil, melted

1 tsp vanilla extract

1 tsp apple cider vinegar

GLAZE

¼ cup [55 g] vegan butter substitute

½ cup [100 g] sugar

2 Tbsp oat milk

2 Tbsp unsweetened cocoa powder

2 tsp vanilla extract

½ tsp cinnamon

TOPPING

Dairy-free vanilla bean ice cream

SERVES 9

This decadent and fudgy vegan chocolate cake is infused with coffee, deepening the chocolate flavor. The pairing is one of my family's favorites; they look forward to it every time I make this and serve it for dessert. There's just something about coffee and chocolate that brings people together—I literally have to keep them out of the kitchen while it cools. If that's not a telltale sign of a great dessert worth sharing, I don't know what is!

TO MAKE THE CAKE:

1. Preheat the oven to 350°F [180°C].

2. Grease an 8 in [20 cm] square baking dish with coconut oil. Use a little cocoa powder to dust the inside of the dish and shake out the excess.

3. In a large bowl, whisk together the flour, sugar, cocoa powder, baking soda, and salt. Add the coffee, coconut oil, vanilla, and apple cider vinegar and whisk until fully combined. The batter will be a bit lumpy. Pour the batter into the prepared baking dish.

4. Bake for 30 to 35 minutes, or until the center of the cake is set.

cont.

NOTE: *Don't be afraid to experiment with the spices in the glaze to complement the chocolate and coffee flavors. Not a cinnamon fan? Try ½ tsp of ground cardamom, or a pinch of ground cayenne for a little heat.*

TO MAKE THE GLAZE:

1. In a small saucepan over medium heat, melt the vegan butter. Add the sugar, oat milk, cocoa powder, vanilla, and cinnamon and whisk continuously until the sugar has dissolved and a smooth glaze forms.

2. Once you pull the cake out of the oven, pour the glaze over the entire cake immediately. It will sink in. Allow the cake to cool for at least 30 minutes.

TO SERVE:

1. Serve warm with lots of vanilla ice cream. Store leftovers in the fridge for up to 2 days.

FOOD FOR THOUGHT:
Relationships are like recipes. They require a pinch of this, a dash of that, and an understanding of how everything works together to make something beautiful.

Want S'mores Cookies?

1 cup [220 g] unsalted butter, melted

1 cup [200 g] packed
light brown sugar

½ cup [100 g] granulated sugar

1 tsp vanilla extract

2 large eggs, at room temperature

2 cups [280 g] all-purpose flour

1 cup [120 g] graham cracker
crumbs (see Note)

1½ tsp kosher salt

1 tsp baking soda

1 tsp ground cinnamon

1½ cups [270 g] semisweet
chocolate chips

¾ cup [45 g] mini marshmallows

NOTE: *If you can't find pre-ground graham cracker crumbs, take 1 sleeve of graham crackers and either grind them in a food processor or put them in a zip-top plastic bag and smash them with a rolling pin.*

MAKES 16 COOKIES

Some of my sweetest memories are of being around a big beach bonfire with friends, having some drinks, sharing stories, and yes, snacking on s'mores. Thankfully, all you need to enjoy these savory, sweet, fire-alarm-free s'mores cookies is your oven and a few good friends or family members.

1. In a large bowl, combine the melted butter, brown sugar, and granulated sugar. Whisk together until well combined.

2. Add the vanilla and the eggs one at a time, whisking together until combined and scraping down the sides as needed with a spatula between each addition.

3. In the same bowl, add the flour, graham cracker crumbs, salt, baking soda, and cinnamon. With a silicone spatula, fold everything together until most of the flour is incorporated.

4. Fold in the chocolate chips until everything is just combined, then cover the mixing bowl with plastic wrap and refrigerate for at least 1 hour. The dough will keep for 7 days in the fridge.

5. Preheat the oven to 375°F [190°C] and line a baking sheet with parchment paper.

cont.

NOTE: *To make vegan, replace the butter, graham cracker crumbs, chocolate chips, and marshmallows with vegan versions. Use flax eggs in place of chicken eggs—mix 1 Tbsp of ground flaxseed with 3 Tbsp room-temperature water per egg and let sit for 10 minutes before adding. Mix and bake cookie dough according to the original method.*

6. Once the dough is chilled, use a ¼ cup [60 ml] ice cream scoop to scoop up six cookies and place them on the baking sheet about 2 in [5 cm] apart. Bake for 5 minutes.

7. Remove the cookies from the oven and press 4 to 6 miniature marshmallows into the center of each cookie.

8. Return the cookies to the oven and bake for another 7 minutes, or until the edges are set, the middle is still soft, and the whole cookie starts to turn golden brown.

9. Remove the cookies from the oven and let them cool on the baking sheet for 5 minutes, then transfer to a wire rack to finish cooling. Repeat with the remaining dough and marshmallows as desired. Store at room temperature in an airtight container for up to 3 days; layer the cookies with parchment or wax paper to keep the marshmallows from sticking.

FOOD FOR THOUGHT:
The key to creating strong bonds is not being afraid and running when things get sticky. It's those messy moments that can bring us closer to others.

Pesto Pull-Apart Bread

¾ cup [180 ml] whole milk, heated to 110°F [45°C]

1 Tbsp sugar

2¼ tsp active dry yeast

1 Tbsp salted butter, at room temperature

1 egg

2⅓ cups [325 g] bread flour

½ tsp table salt

1 tsp garlic powder

1 tsp dried Italian seasoning

½ cup [120 g] pesto

½ cup [15 g] shredded Parmesan cheese

1 Tbsp extra-virgin olive oil

½ cup [30 g] freshly shredded Asiago cheese

SERVES 12

Plain dinner rolls? Boring! During big family Saturday luncheons, my mother would make a pesto dipping sauce with fresh basil from her garden. This pesto bread is my tribute to her and those lunches with my family, and it will put regular rolls to shame. Just set this loaf at the center of the table during any gathering, and watch everyone dive right in.

1. In a small bowl, combine the warm milk, sugar, and yeast. Set aside for 10 minutes while the yeast activates.

2. In the bowl of a stand mixer fitted with the paddle attachment, or in a medium bowl using a handheld electric mixer, beat the butter and egg for 1 minute. Add the yeast mixture and continue mixing for 30 seconds.

3. If your mixer has a dough hook attachment, attach it now. Don't worry if you don't; the regular beaters will work just fine. Add the flour, salt, garlic powder, and Italian seasoning. Mix on low speed until a sticky dough forms and begins to pull away from the sides of the bowl.

4. Turn out the dough onto a lightly floured surface and knead until the dough is smooth and elastic, 5 to 8 minutes. Place the dough in a lightly oiled bowl and cover with a damp cloth. Set the dough aside to rise for 90 minutes, or until it doubles in size.

cont.

5. Grease an 8 by 4 in [20 by 10 cm] loaf pan with butter.

6. Punch down the dough and divide it into twelve equal pieces. Use your hands to work each piece into roughly 6 in [15 cm] squares. Spread the pesto onto each square and sprinkle shredded Parmesan cheese over the pesto. Fold each square of dough in half, with the pesto and cheese on the inside.

7. Nestle each piece of dough into the prepared pan, folded edges touching the bottom and open edges pointing upward. Repeat with the remaining pieces until the pan is full and you have a makeshift loaf. Re-cover the dough and set it aside to rise for another 45 minutes.

8. Preheat the oven to 350°F [180°C].

9. Uncover the loaf and bake for 40 minutes.

10. Remove the bread from the oven and use a pastry brush to brush the tops with the olive oil and sprinkle on the Asiago cheese. Bake for 10 minutes more.

11. Let cool in the pan for 10 minutes before removing. Serve immediately to a big table of friends and family.

BAKING AFFIRMATION:
My kitchen is a safe place to connect. I trust my voice—and my taste buds.

Take Me to Chocolate Heaven Cookies

3 cups [360 g] powdered sugar

⅔ cup [50 g] unsweetened cocoa powder

½ tsp fine sea salt

4 egg whites

2 tsp vanilla extract

⅔ cup [120 g] mini chocolate chips or chopped chocolate

NOTE: *For those who keep kosher for passover, this is a great way to break up the large amounts of matzoh consumed during the week.*

FOOD FOR THOUGHT:
The more time passes, the more daunting it feels to connect with people. Make the time—even if you only have a minute or two—to check in and say hello.

MAKES 20 COOKIES

You know that friend from work who is allergic to gluten? Or wait, was it soy? Mangoes, maybe? Guess what? It doesn't matter! This flourless cookie is perfect to whip up in times of doubt. This is another recipe from my mother, which automatically means it's delicious (we can't be friends if you disagree). Make sure to use good-quality cocoa powder for the richest, fudgiest, chewiest cookies.

1. Preheat the oven to 350°F [180°C]. Line three baking sheets with parchment paper and spray the parchment paper with nonstick cooking spray. Set aside.

2. In a large bowl, mix the powdered sugar, cocoa powder, and salt. Add the egg whites and vanilla and whisk until a thick and smooth batter forms. It will look a little like brownie batter. Fold in the chocolate chips.

3. Using a cookie scoop (about 2 Tbsp), scoop the batter onto the prepared baking sheet. The cookies spread a lot, so I usually bake six on each sheet.

4. Bake one or two sheets at a time for 10 to 12 minutes, or until the tops of the cookies look shiny and there are visible cracks on them. Let cool completely and then carefully peel the parchment paper away from the bottoms of the cookies.

5. Store at room temperature for up to 3 days.

Limoncello Tiramisu in a Glass

CUSTARD

¾ cup [180 ml] heavy cream

1 lb [455 g] mascarpone,
at room temperature

Two 12 oz [340 g] jars lemon curd

¼ cup [50 g] granulated sugar

2 tsp grated lemon zest,
plus more for topping

LIMONCELLO LADYFINGERS

¾ cup [180 ml] limoncello

2 Tbsp fresh lemon juice

One 7 oz [200 g] package
crispy ladyfingers

TOPPING

¾ cup [90 g] fresh raspberries

SERVES 6

Want to sweeten things up in the kitchen? This twist on tiramisu is perfect for couples who want to work on their teamwork—and communication—skills. After all, more hands make less work. You can divvy up the steps: You dip, I'll layer, we'll make the sauce. It all comes together in the end in one cohesive, beautiful dessert. On your next date night, cozy up and head to the kitchen together.

TO MAKE THE CUSTARD:

1. In the bowl of a stand mixer fitted with the whisk attachment, or in a medium bowl using a handheld electric mixer, beat the heavy cream until stiff peaks form.

2. In a medium bowl, with the stand mixer or using a handheld electric mixer, beat the mascarpone until smooth. Add one jar of the lemon curd, the sugar, and the lemon zest and stir to combine. Mix one-fourth of the whipped cream into the mascarpone mixture to lighten it and then fold in the remaining cream with a silicone spatula.

TO MAKE THE LIMONCELLO LADYFINGERS:

1. In a shallow bowl, stir together the limoncello, lemon juice, and 3 Tbsp of water. Cut the ladyfingers to fit into six serving glasses, such as wineglasses, clear mugs, or shallow bowls. If the ladyfingers are too big to fit, feel free to break them up.

cont.

NOTE: *The key ingredient here is the ladyfingers—choose the crispy ones (not the soft ones) that can hold up to the soaking step. And use room-temperature mascarpone so it is easier to stir. If you can't find crispy ladyfingers, buy two 3 oz [85 g] packages of soft ladyfingers, separate them on a parchment-lined baking sheet, and bake at 250°F [120°C] for 15 to 20 minutes, or until they start to crisp. They'll continue to dry out as they cool.*

2. Dip each side of the ladyfingers into the limoncello mixture. Don't leave them in the liquid too long or they will fall apart. Layer the custard mixture, then dipped ladyfingers, then drizzle the lemon curd from the remaining jar into the glasses until you reach the top. As long as you get all the components into each glass, there is no wrong way to do this.

TO SERVE:

1. Decorate the top with fresh raspberries or lemon zest—or both—and cover with plastic wrap. Chill in the fridge for at least 2 hours before serving.

BAKING AFFIRMATION:
I treasure my ability to communicate with others. The whole is greater than the sum of its parts.

Cookies and Cream Brownies

BROWNIE LAYER

1 cup [140 g] all-purpose flour

1 cup [80 g] cocoa powder

1 tsp fine sea salt

Pinch of espresso powder, or ¼ tsp cofee extract

¾ cup [165 g] unsalted butter

2 oz [55 g] semisweet chocolate, chopped

2 cups [400 g] granulated sugar

3 eggs, at room temperature

2 tsp vanilla extract

13 or 14 Oreos, chopped

COOKIES AND CREAM TOPPING

2 cups [360 g] white chocolate chips

6 Tbsp [90 ml] heavy cream

¼ cup [30 g] powdered sugar

12 Oreos, chopped

MAKES 15 BROWNIES

We all have different ways of eating Oreos. A personal favorite is to share a cookie with someone—twisting the sandwich cookie apart as if it were a wishbone to see who gets the side with the most cream. Well, thankfully you don't have to fight over that with these cookies and cream brownies. This recipe has Oreos in every fudgy, chocolatey bite, so the only disagreement should be over who gets the last one.

TO MAKE THE BROWNIE LAYER:

1. Preheat the oven to 350°F [180°C]. Coat a 9 by 13 in [23 by 33 cm] baking pan with nonstick cooking spray, line with parchment, then spray again. Set the pan aside.

2. In a medium bowl, whisk the flour, cocoa powder, salt, and espresso (if using instead of coffee extract) and set aside.

3. In a large microwave-safe bowl, combine the butter and chocolate and heat in 20-second increments, stirring after each round, until it is totally melted and smooth. Alternatively, you can melt it in a double boiler on the stove. Add the granulated sugar to the chocolate mixture and stir to combine. Stir in the eggs, one at a time, then add the vanilla and coffee extract (if using in place of espresso powder) and mix again.

cont.

NOTE: *Don't overmix the brownie batter. It will result in tough brownies.*

4. Add the dry ingredients to the chocolate mixture and stir until well combined. Add the chopped Oreos and stir again.

5. Spread the batter into the prepared pan and smooth the top with an offset spatula. The batter will be very thick. Bake for 25 to 28 minutes, or until a toothpick inserted into the center comes out clean. Set the brownies aside to cool.

TO MAKE THE TOPPING:

1. In a microwave-safe bowl, combine the white chocolate chips and heavy cream and heat in 20-second increments until it is melted and smooth. Add the powdered sugar and Oreos and mix again. Spread the mixture on the cooled brownies.

TO SERVE:

1. Cut the cooled brownies into fifteen squares. Store leftover brownies in an airtight container for up to 5 days.

FOOD FOR THOUGHT:
While your baked goods are in the oven, take turns sharing three things you appreciate about your partner, child, or friend.

Warm Cornbread Muffins

WITH HOT HONEY BUTTER

2¼ cup [315 g] all-purpose flour

1 cup [140 g] cornmeal

¾ cup [150 g] sugar

½ cup [70 g] cornstarch

2 tsp baking powder

1¼ tsp baking soda

1 tsp fine sea salt

¼ tsp nutmeg (optional)

1 cup [240 ml] whole milk

1 cup [240 g] sour cream

⅔ cup [160 g] canola
or vegetable oil

2 eggs

⅓ cup [115 g] honey

Hot Honey Butter (recipe
follows), for serving

MAKES 12 MUFFINS

Muffins are the most versatile baked good out there. They're perfect for introducing yourself to the neighbors or bringing to the charitable bake sale. And they're so comforting! You can have them for breakfast, as a snack, or honestly, even as dessert. What makes this recipe my new favorite for corn muffins (they've always been my favorite) is the hot honey butter that's served on the side. It's a sweet kick to your taste buds, but sure to add a little spice to a connection with someone else.

1. Line a standard muffin tin with paper liners and set aside.

2. In a large bowl, combine the flour, cornmeal, sugar, cornstarch, baking powder, baking soda, salt, and nutmeg (if using).

3. In another bowl, combine the milk, sour cream, oil, eggs, and honey. Using a silicone spatula, add the wet ingredients to the dry ingredients and fold with a silicone spatula until just blended (if you overmix here, you will get tough muffins). If you have time and want bakery-style domed tops, put the muffin batter in the fridge for 1 hour.

4. Preheat the oven to 375°F [190°C].

cont.

NOTE: *Remember that hot honey is a component to be mixed with the butter, not to be eaten separately!*

¼ cup [85 g] honey

½ cup [110 g] unsalted butter, at room temperature, cut into chunks

2 tsp hot sauce

Pinch of kosher salt

FOOD FOR THOUGHT:
Take comfort in comforting others! It's a wonderful way to serve up some deliciously warm treats and make connections all at once.

5. Using a large cookie scoop, divide the muffin batter among the muffin paper liners, filling the batter all the way to the top. Bake for 20 to 22 minutes, or until golden brown.

6. Let cool in the pan for 5 minutes, then flip out onto a cooling rack to cool completely.

7. Serve with the hot honey butter. Store leftovers in the fridge for up to 2 days.

Hot Honey Butter

1. In a microwave-safe bowl, heat the honey in 20-second increments until it is smooth and easy to stir. Add the butter, hot sauce, and salt and mix thoroughly. Store leftovers in the fridge for up to 2 weeks.

Let's Go on a Date(-Stuffed) Cookies

FILLING

1 lb [455 g] Medjool dates, pitted

1 cup [120 g] walnuts, chopped

1 tsp orange blossom water

COOKIES

2 cups [280 g] all-purpose flour

1 cup [160 g] semolina flour

½ cup [100 g] packed
light brown sugar

1 tsp ground cinnamon

½ tsp ground coriander

½ tsp ground cardamom

1 tsp table salt

1 cup [220 g] unsalted butter,
at room temperature

½ to ¾ cup [120 to 180 ml] warm
water, about 110°F [45°C]

1 tsp rose water

Powdered sugar, for dusting

MAKES 40 COOKIES

Talk about beautiful little delights. My Great-Aunt Renee
is famous in the community for this cookie recipe. They're
excellent for when you want to jazz things up a bit for a
big get-together or fancy party. Just remember that when
you shape the cookies, you need to be gentle with them
in the same way you should be gentle with your relationships. If you squeeze too hard, they break. If you handle
them with care, something beautiful will emerge.

TO MAKE THE FILLING:

1. In a medium saucepan, add the dates and just
   enough water to cover. Bring to a boil, then lower the
   heat to a simmer. Simmer the dates for 20 minutes, or
   until they are softened. Do not drain any remaining
   water. Use a fork or potato masher to mash the dates
   into a paste, then add the walnuts and orange blossom water. Stir well to combine and set aside to cool.

TO MAKE THE COOKIES:

1. Preheat the oven to 350°F [180°C].

2. In a large bowl, whisk the flours, brown sugar, cinnamon, coriander, cardamon, and salt. Add the butter
   and use a handheld electric mixer on low speed to
   combine. The butter will not fully incorporate, and
   you will end up with a crumbly mixture. Don't worry!

3. Add ¼ cup [60 ml] of the warm water and the rose
   water. Mix on low speed for 30 seconds, then add

   cont.

another ¼ cup [60 ml] of warm water and continue to mix until well incorporated.

4. Use your hands to knead the dough together into a ball. If the dough is too dry to fully incorporate the dry ingredients, add the remaining warm water, 1 Tbsp at a time, until the dough comes together.

5. Cut the dough in half and turn each dough portion out onto a lightly floured surface. Use a rolling pin to roll the dough out to ¼ in [6 mm] thickness. Use a 3 in [7.5 cm] cookie cutter to cut rounds out of the dough. Gather the scraps, re-roll the dough, and cut out more rounds until all the dough has been used.

6. Place 2 tsp of the filling into the center of each round, spreading it horizontally into a strip. Use your fingers to gently bring the top and bottom edges of the cookie together, forming a tube shape around the filling.

7. Place the cookies on an ungreased baking sheet and bake for 15 minutes, or until they begin to turn golden. Remove them from the oven and allow to cool completely.

8. Dust the cookies with powdered sugar just before serving. Store leftovers in the fridge for up to 3 days.

FOOD FOR THOUGHT:
Baking requires some TLC: trust, letting go, and composure. Try applying that thinking to your most intimate relationships.

Syrian Carrot Cake

CAKE

2½ cups [350 g] all-purpose flour

1 cup [200 g] granulated sugar

¾ cup [150 g] packed
light brown sugar

2 tsp baking powder

2 tsp baking soda

1 tsp table salt

1 tsp ground cinnamon

1 tsp ground coriander

½ tsp ground cardamom

¼ tsp ground nutmeg

1 cup [120 g] pecans, chopped

4 large dates, pitted and chopped

1 lb [455 g] carrots,
peeled and grated

1 cup [240 ml] canola oil

4 eggs

¾ cup [180 g] sour cream

2 tsp vanilla extract

SERVES 8 TO 10

Everyone knows what carrot cake is all about, but this recipe is a super-unique twist on that classic. You see, most carrot cakes use raisins—but Syrians use dates instead! Dates provide natural sweetness and give a deeper flavor dimension to whatever you're baking. And they have a low glycemic index, which makes this carrot cake a little more guilt-free. It's perfectly sweet, without too much sweetness; others will surely love it too.

TO MAKE THE CAKE:

1. Preheat the oven to 350°F [180°C]. Coat three 8 in [20 cm] round cake pans with nonstick cooking spray.

2. In a large bowl, whisk the flour, sugars, baking powder, baking soda, salt, cinnamon, coriander, cardamon, and nutmeg until well combined. Add the pecans and dates and stir to coat with the flour mixture. Use a wooden spoon to stir in the grated carrots.

3. In a medium bowl, use a handheld electric mixer to beat the oil, eggs, sour cream, and vanilla until well combined. Add to the dry ingredients and stir with a wooden spoon until just combined.

4. Divide the batter evenly among the pans and smooth the tops with an offset spatula.

FROSTING

1 lb [455 g] cream cheese,
at room temperature

1½ cups [330 g] unsalted butter,
at room temperature

1 tsp vanilla extract

1 tsp almond extract

½ tsp fresh lemon juice

½ tsp table salt

3 cups [360 g] powdered
sugar, sifted

5. Bake for 40 minutes, or until a toothpick inserted into the center of each cake comes out clean. Remove the cakes from the oven and set them on cooling racks. Allow to cool completely.

TO MAKE THE FROSTING AND ASSEMBLE:

1. In a large bowl, use a handheld electric mixer or a stand mixer with the paddle attachment to beat the cream cheese and butter until fluffy, then beat in the vanilla, almond extract, lemon juice, and salt. Add the powdered sugar, 1 cup [120 g] at a time, and beat until the frosting is fluffy and light. Cover the frosting and set it aside until the cakes are ready to frost.

2. Remove the cakes from their pans by flipping them upside down and slamming them onto a flat surface. Shave the tops off of each cake with a serrated knife and spread a layer of icing over each leveled cake. Stack the cakes, then frost as desired. Feel free to use a piping bag to decorate! Store leftovers in the fridge for up to 2 days.

BAKING AFFIRMATION:
I'm committed to being an open communicator and an active listener.

Finding Joy

I'm so happy you're here! If you haven't noticed, the outcome of all the guidance from the previous chapters culminates in a central theme: finding joy or happiness. Self-Care (page 22) helps you put yourself first, because, as the flight attendants tell us, we need to put our own oxygen mask on before helping others. Mindfulness (page 56) allows you to center yourself and tune out distractions. Finding Comfort (page 96) helps you experience solace when life seems overwhelming. Dealing with Stress and Anxiety (page 130) lets you focus on the good things in your life. Letting Go of Frustration (page 166) allows you to relax into the present moment. And Connecting with Others (page 200) in an authentic way creates deeper and stronger bonds. The secret? Baking is a joyful experience. Good food = happiness.

That feeling of happiness can come from external factors, such as a compliment from a friend, or internally, like waking up with gratitude. Both are important, but the best kind of happiness comes from within—it's a powerful feeling we generate. When we rely on others for our happiness, we set ourselves up for disappointment because we are relying on validation to find our own self-worth. (I like to describe this as "validation-shopping" and there's a very strict return policy.) It leads to a happiness high, with an eventual crash after. That's why social media can be so problematic. We believe the content we share is a representation of ourselves, and the likes and comments are a reflection of that. But the reality is, it's not. Let them doom-scroll and go on a double-tap frenzy. Your worth is not tied to the number of likes you receive.

I'll let you in on another secret: Happiness "doesn't come standard." Unlike the dealership showroom car, happiness is personalized; it's based on your interests, your activities, and yes, even the flavors or foods you love. This is why some people identify as beach bums and others as snow bunnies. Or why people reach for savory snacks versus sweet treats.

The definition of happiness is sometimes too ethereal to understand. One of my favorite professors offered up a twist, what he called "the art of not being unhappy." It can be a lot of work to make sure you're happy. Constantly chasing those happiness highs? It's exhausting. Not being unhappy is appreciating the smaller things, or not waiting for a "grand gesture" of happiness, like winning the lottery.

This approach is something I try to instill in my patients. They tend to suffer from the "bigger, better, best" next thing mentality. There's a paradox of choice, where we take even the simplest of things that once gave us happiness and are suddenly not happy with them because there's another "shiny object" we're attracted to. The same goes for relationships. And that's why dating in NYC is a nightmare!

Look, I am no Dalai Lama (though I do look great in a robe), but I can honestly say from my experience as both a New Yorker and a psychologist that true joy can't be bought. It can, however, be baked! I've definitely come across people who are truly joyful in their lives, experience something like a perpetual happiness. I wonder how many of them love baking—like, really love baking. Or as I call it, "Joy Baking."

Joy Baking is an effortless way to find happiness. It unleashes our inner child and stirs up memories of favorite treats. It allows us to be creative—which is especially great if your 9-to-5 is just blah. The baking tools we use are magic wands, transforming ingredients. The baking techniques can awaken the body, like a mini workout, but without dropping dead in a puddle of your own sweat in an exercise class. Whisking flour is a mini endorphin rush. Baking awakens our senses.

So what brings you joy in the kitchen? For me, it's sneaking a bit of the batter, my favorite childhood pastime. Licking the spoon. Watching the stiff peaks of meringue form from sticky egg whites. Or adding that extra scoop of chocolate chips into the dough (and maybe into your mouth). Don't forget the tantalizing aroma of sugar cookies emanating from the oven. It's heaven!

We have so much to celebrate, especially in the kitchen. Whether it's the ingredients in front of us coming together beautifully or trying new flavors and recipes, we're creating a joyful moment—and then putting that joy back into our bodies when we take the first bite. You'll be surprised at what new recipes and flavors can do. My Golden Tres Leches Cake (page 258) is a Guatemalan specialty that uses golden milk and was passed down to me by my Abuela Raquel. The star ingredient is turmeric, which is known to give a boost of energy.

Coffee is a natural stimulant; it wakes you up. Chocolate gives you a bit of a "high" (more so when you eat the whole bar). These ingredients can impact the joy we get from food. So do the final touches, like frosting, sprinkles, and the rich colors of baked goods.

The truth is, happiness is contagious. From bringing us joy in the kitchen, to the smile on friends' faces when we share with them, making others feel good makes us feel good. More simply, "Sharing is caring," as they say. It can be as small as a Rainbow Pride Cupcake (page 265) or it can be something bigger, like this cookbook. Creating this book was a labor of love, and I couldn't be happier for pushing myself. But telling my family and friends about it? The smile I had on my face and seeing theirs filled me with joy.

It reminds me of one Jackism I tell my patients: "Don't be a white potato." Their faces usually scrunch up, confused at the phrase. White potatoes are like a sponge; they absorb everything. If you're a white potato, you're just going to absorb energy without giving anything back. Happiness is contagious and meant to be shared. Give that energy back into the world. That's why cupcakes come in dozens.

The next time you need a little mood boost, grab one of these recipes and head into the kitchen. Find the moments in—and out of—the kitchen that bring you joy. It will nourish your mind, body, and soul. Happy baking!

Quick Session
YOUR RECIPE FOR HAPPINESS

Sitting down with patients—whether it's their first session or not—always yields an interesting conversation around "finding happiness." I'll ask, "What do you want?" Nine times out of ten, their response is, "I just want to be happy." They feel like happiness is always out of reach.

"If only I could find a partner." "If only we could have kids." "If only I was able to live where I wanted to." "If only I didn't have to constantly take care of my parents and could enjoy a bit more of my individual life." But I've found that they seldom talk about what happiness looks like.

In my clinical experience, joy exists inside of us, and we just have to unlock it. One patient was really struggling with this concept, so I gave them a bit of homework to do. I asked if they had ever heard of a gratitude jar. The concept is relatively simple: Write down one thing each day that made you happy or proud. It could be anything. Place that small piece of paper into a jar and seal it up. As the days turn into weeks and into months, the number of gratitudes will grow. After four months of sessions, I asked them to bring the gratitude jar in.

During that session I asked them to reach in and grab one piece of paper to read. A small smile creeped in. Another brought about a little chuckle and a smirk. That's the beauty of the gratitude jar. It randomizes those joyful events so you can surprise yourself with all the good you've experienced over time. Each little piece of paper is an ingredient for happiness, and you had them inside of you all along.

Confetti Pound Cake

1¾ cups [350 g] sugar

1 cup [220 g] unsalted butter, at room temperature

3 eggs plus 3 egg yolks

½ cup [120 g] sour cream

1 Tbsp vanilla extract

1¾ cups [245 g] all-purpose flour

1 tsp fine sea salt

6 Tbsp [65 g] rainbow sprinkles

Homemade Whipped Cream (page 39), for serving

MAKES 2 LOAVES

Take a boring pound cake and add joy with vibrant sprinkles. While baking can be fussy, you don't need any expensive or unusual ingredients for this recipe, and you probably already have most, if not all, of them in your pantry. Plus, this recipe makes two loaves, so you can keep one for yourself and share the other at a small gathering.

1. Preheat the oven to 350°F [180°C]. Grease two 8 by 4 in [20 by 10 cm] loaf pans with 1 Tbsp of vegetable shortening. Coat the insides of the pans with flour and tap out the excess.

2. In the bowl of a stand mixer fitted with the paddle attachment, or in a large bowl using a handheld electric mixer, beat the sugar and butter until fluffy. Add the eggs and egg yolks, one at a time, mixing well after each addition. Add the sour cream and vanilla, then mix on medium-high speed for about 1 minute.

3. Add the flour and salt to the bowl and mix on low speed, periodically using a rubber spatula to scrape down the sides of the bowl. A thick and smooth batter should form fairly quickly. At this point, add the sprinkles and mix until just incorporated.

4. Distribute the batter evenly between the two pre-pared pans and place them on a baking sheet.

cont.

5. Bake for 45 minutes to 1 hour, or until a cake tester comes out clean and the sides pull away from the pan.

6. Allow the cakes to cool in their pans for 20 minutes before gently removing and transferring to a wire cooling rack. Allow to cool for at least another 20 minutes.

7. Slice and serve with whipped cream. Store leftovers in the fridge for up to 2 days.

FOOD FOR THOUGHT:
The sweetest things in life come to those who wait. Happiness can't be rushed.

Manifesting Cookie Bars

CRUST

2 tsp ground flaxseed

½ cup [110 g] salted butter

¼ cup [50 g] granulated sugar

¼ cup [20 g] unsweetened cocoa powder

1 tsp vanilla extract

1¾ cups [210 g] graham cracker crumbs

½ cup [60 g] almond slivers, finely chopped

½ cup [40 g] unsweetened shredded coconut

FILLING

¼ cup [20 g] powdered milk

3 Tbsp heavy cream

1 tsp vanilla extract

½ cup [110 g] unsalted butter, at room temperature

1½ cups [180 g] powdered sugar

MAKES 16 BARS

Since these bars are no-bake, you'll have a lot of downtime while each layer sets in the fridge. I call these Manifesting Cookie Bars, because I love the idea of challenging yourself to set a joyful intention while you prepare, spread, and chill. Fill the rest of that time with things you enjoy: a TV show, a board game, a really good book, or even another recipe.

TO MAKE THE CRUST:

1. Grease an 8 in [20 cm] square baking pan with 1 tsp coconut oil. If you want, you can also line the bottom with parchment paper.

2. In a small bowl, combine the flaxseed with 1 tsp of water and set aside for 5 minutes.

3. In a small saucepan, melt the butter over low heat. Add the granulated sugar and cocoa powder. Turn the heat up to medium and whisk continuously until the sugar is dissolved and the ingredients are well combined. Remove the pan from heat and stir in the flax mixture and vanilla.

4. In a medium bowl, combine the graham cracker crumbs, almonds, and shredded coconut. Pour the butter mixture over the top and toss until well coated. Use your hands to press this mixture into the bottom of the prepared baking pan, keeping every-thing as even as possible. Refrigerate.

TOPPING

1 cup [180 g] semisweet
chocolate chips

3 Tbsp unsalted butter,
cut into small pieces

TO MAKE THE FILLING:

1. In the bowl of a stand mixer fitted with the paddle attachment, or in a medium bowl using a handheld electric mixer, beat the powdered milk, cream, and vanilla until completely dissolved. Add the butter and beat to combine. At this stage, the mixture may look separated. Add the powdered sugar and mix on low speed until everything is well combined and smooth, then bump the mixer up to medium-high and beat until fluffy.

2. Remove the crust from the fridge and spread the filling evenly over the top, making sure there is no space between the filling and the sides of the baking dish. Return to the fridge.

TO MAKE THE TOPPING AND SERVE:

1. Place the chocolate chips and butter in a microwave-safe bowl. Make sure that the bowl is completely dry, as any water will cause the chocolate to seize. Microwave the chocolate mixture in 15-second intervals, stirring after each one, until the chocolate and butter are completely melted. Leave the bowl at room temperature to cool, coming back to stir it occasionally.

2. Once the chocolate is cool, remove the baking dish from the fridge and spread the chocolate layer over the filling, again making sure to leave no space between the chocolate and the sides. Refrigerate again for 20 minutes, or until the chocolate layer is somewhat set. It will not completely harden.

3. Slice the bars into sixteen squares and serve immediately or keep cool until ready to serve. Store leftovers in the fridge for up to 4 days.

Lemon and Lavender Cookies

COOKIES

¾ cup [150 g] granulated sugar

½ cup [110 g] unsalted butter, at room temperature

1 egg, at room temperature

⅓ cup [80 g] ricotta cheese

1 tsp vanilla extract

2¼ cups [315 g] all-purpose flour

1½ tsp cornstarch

1 tsp culinary-grade dried lavender flowers, ground or finely chopped

½ tsp baking powder

½ tsp baking soda

¼ tsp cream of tartar

Pinch of table salt

FROSTING

½ cup [110 g] unsalted butter, at room temperature

2½ cups [300 g] powdered sugar

1 tsp vanilla extract

2 Tbsp half-and-half

1½ tsp fresh lemon juice

cont.

MAKES 25 COOKIES

The goal of a really great cookie is one that everyone in the family can enjoy eating, like these fragrant and pretty cookies. And that pile of buttercream on top? That's joy in a spoonful.

TO MAKE THE COOKIES:

1. In the bowl of a stand mixer fitted with the paddle attachment, or in a medium bowl using a handheld electric mixer, beat the granulated sugar and butter until fluffy. Add the egg, ricotta, and vanilla and mix until creamy, scraping down the sides of the bowl with a rubber spatula as you go.

2. In a separate bowl, combine the flour, cornstarch, lavender, baking powder, baking soda, cream of tartar, and salt. Set your mixer to low, add the flour mixture, and beat until a very sticky batter comes together. Cover the bowl and allow the batter to chill in the fridge for 1 hour.

TO MAKE THE FROSTING:

1. In the bowl of a stand mixer fitted with the whisk attachment, or in a large bowl using a hand-held electric mixer, cream the butter until light and fluffy. Add one-third of the powdered sugar and the vanilla and beat to combine. Continue adding the sugar in thirds until it has all been used, starting at a low speed and working up to medium until the sugar is well blended. The frosting won't be super creamy yet, but that's OK!

cont.

TOPPINGS

Culinary-grade dried lavender flowers (see Note)

Grated lemon zest

NOTE: *Sprinkle the lavender flowers as a topping very lightly. Too much lavender leads to a soapy flavor, and no one wants to eat soap.*

FOOD FOR THOUGHT:
Happiness isn't cookie cutter. What brings you happiness may not be the same for someone else. It's OK to have your happiness come from different sources than others.

2. Add the half-and-half and lemon juice and beat on medium-high speed. A fluffy buttercream should form in a minute or two. Set the frosting aside in the fridge.

TO BAKE AND FROST THE COOKIES:

1. Preheat the oven to 375°F [190°C]. Line two baking sheets with parchment paper.

2. Roll the cookie dough out about 1/16 in [2 mm] thick. Use any cookie cutter that brings you joy to cut out each cookie. Place the shaped cookies on the prepared baking sheets.

3. Bake for 10 to 12 minutes, or until the edges of the cookies just begin to turn golden. Let cool completely on the baking sheets. This will finish baking the cookies.

4. Fit a piping bag with the piping tip of your choice and fill with the frosting. Pipe a nice, thick layer of frosting on top of the cookies. You want the edges to be bare, so keep most of the frosting toward the middle; do this by starting in the center of the cookies and spiraling outward as you pipe.

5. Sprinkle the cookies with the lavender and lemon zest. Serve immediately or leave them uncovered on the counter for a few hours to harden the frosting a bit. Store leftovers in the fridge for up to 3 days.

Grapefruit White Chocolate Yogurt Cake

CAKE

1½ cups [210 g] all-purpose flour

2 tsp baking powder

½ tsp baking soda

½ tsp fine sea salt

¾ cup [150 g] granulated sugar

1 medium grapefruit

2 eggs

1 cup [240 g] plain full-fat
yogurt (see Note)

½ cup [120 ml] canola
or vegetable oil

1 tsp vanilla extract

¼ tsp coconut extract (optional)

½ cup [90 g] white chocolate chips

GLAZE

1 medium grapefruit

1 cup [120 g] powdered sugar,
plus more as needed

Pinch of salt

2 Tbsp toasted unsweetened
shredded coconut

SERVES 10

Seasonal depression (a.k.a. seasonal affective disorder) is a very real struggle for many people. Winter can make us feel less than fabulous. But a great way to boost your mood is to invite summer into every aspect of your life by making this luscious cake. With yogurt for probiotics and vitamin C for those dreary winter months, this moist cake will bring a sunny note to your kitchen—and your taste buds.

TO MAKE THE CAKE:

1. Preheat the oven to 350°F [180°C]. Butter or spray a 9 by 5 in [23 by 12 cm] loaf pan. Line the bottom with parchment paper, leaving overhang on the sides. Set aside.

2. In a medium bowl, whisk together the flour, baking powder, baking soda, and salt.

3. Put the granulated sugar in a large bowl. Use a microplane to zest the grapefruit directly over the sugar, then use clean fingers to rub the zest into the sugar until it is fragrant. Juice the grapefruit (you will need ¼ cup [60 ml] of juice) and set the juice aside. Add the eggs to the sugar and whisk until pale and foamy, about 1 minute. Add the yogurt, oil, grapefruit juice, vanilla, and coconut extract, if using, to the sugar mixture and whisk until emulsified.

cont.

4. Stir the flour mixture into the wet ingredients, whisking gently, leaving a few streaks of flour unincorporated. Use a spatula to fold in the white chocolate chips until just combined.

5. Pour the batter into the prepared loaf pan and bake for 50 to 60 minutes, or until the center is set and a toothpick inserted into the center comes out clean. If the cake starts to brown on top, cover it with foil and continue baking.

6. Let the cake cool in the pan for 10 minutes, then remove it gently and set it on a cooling rack to cool completely.

TO MAKE THE GLAZE:

1. Zest and juice the grapefruit and set the zest and juice aside. In a large bowl, whisk the powdered sugar, 2 Tbsp of the grapefruit juice, 1 tsp of the grapefruit zest, and the salt until smooth. If it is too thick, add a drop or two of grapefruit juice. If it is too wet, add 1 tsp of powdered sugar. Slowly pour it over the cake with a small spoon. Top with shredded coconut.

TO SERVE:

1. Let the icing set for 20 minutes, then slice and serve. Store leftovers in the fridge for up to 2 days.

BAKING AFFIRMATION:
I welcome happiness with open arms—and an open stomach.

Cinnamon Chocolate Chip Crumb Muffins

MUFFINS

¾ cup [150 g] granulated sugar

6 Tbsp [90 g] unsalted butter, at room temperature

2 eggs, at room temperature

⅔ cup [160 g] sour cream

1 tsp vanilla extract

1¼ cups [175 g] all-purpose flour

1 tsp ground cinnamon

1 tsp baking powder

½ tsp table salt

¼ tsp baking soda

¾ cup [135 g] semisweet chocolate chips

CRUMB TOPPING

1⅓ cups [185 g] all-purpose flour

½ cup [113 g] unsalted butter, melted

⅓ cup [65 g] packed light brown sugar

¼ cup [50 g] granulated sugar

½ tsp vanilla extract

½ tsp ground cinnamon

Pinch of ground nutmeg

MAKES 12 MUFFINS

You guessed it, another crumb recipe! Trust me, it's totally worth it. Cinnamon and chocolate are delicious ingredients when used separately. But combined, they're heavenly. Lord only knows why (and I'm not one to argue). These muffins are great for breakfast or as an afternoon snack, and even better to make when you've got company to feed.

TO MAKE THE MUFFINS:

1. Preheat the oven to 350°F [180°C]. Line two muffin pans with paper liners and set aside.

2. In the bowl of a stand mixer fitted with the paddle attachment, or in a large bowl using a handheld electric mixer, beat the granulated sugar and butter until fluffy. Decrease the speed to low and add the eggs one at a time, beating after each addition. Add the sour cream and vanilla and beat until well combined.

3. In a separate medium bowl, whisk together the flour, cinnamon, baking powder, salt, and baking soda. With the mixer on low, begin adding the flour mixture to the butter mixture a little at a time. Scrape down the sides of the bowl as needed and mix until you have a consistent and smooth batter. Use a rubber spatula to fold in the chocolate chips.

4. Pour the batter into the muffin liners until they are two-thirds of the way full and set aside.

cont.

TO MAKE THE CRUMB TOPPING:

1. In a medium bowl, combine the flour, butter, brown sugar, granulated sugar, vanilla, cinnamon, and nutmeg and use your fingers to work everything together until you have a crumbly mixture with both large and small pieces. Top the muffins liberally with the crumb mixture.

TO BAKE AND SERVE:

1. Bake for 30 to 35 minutes, or until a toothpick inserted into the center comes out with only a few crumbs. Let cool for 5 minutes before transferring to a wire cooling rack. Enjoy them warm or save them for later. Store leftovers in the fridge for up to 2 days.

FOOD FOR THOUGHT:
Making a crumb topping allows us to use our fingers to play with our food and let go of some of the pressures of adulthood. When you make these muffins, give your inner child a chance to come out and play.

Twix Tart

CRUST

1½ cups [210 g] all-purpose flour

½ cup [60 g] powdered sugar

½ tsp fine sea salt

9 Tbsp [135 g] unsalted butter, cut into small chunks

1 egg yolk

CARAMEL FILLING

½ cup [120 ml] plus 2 Tbsp heavy cream

1 cup [200 g] granulated sugar

2 Tbsp light corn syrup

2 Tbsp unsalted butter, at room temperature

TOPPING

Half a batch Chocolate Ganache (page 30)

SERVES 12

Who doesn't love Twix? Um, nobody. With chocolate, caramel, and a crisp cookie, this tart has something for everyone. And if you like all three, you're in luck. This tart reminds me of coming home from summer camp and rushing to grab a Twix ice cream bar from the freezer. Instant joy!

TO MAKE THE CRUST:

1. Put the flour, powdered sugar, and salt in a food processor and pulse until combined. Add the chunks of butter and pulse until the butter is the size of peas and covered in flour.

2. In a small bowl, mix the egg yolk with 1 Tbsp of ice water. Add the egg mixture to the processer and pulse until the dough forms larger clumps.

3. Transfer the dough to a 9 in [23 cm] square tart pan, or a tart pan with a similar volume, and press into an even layer on the bottom and up the sides. Freeze for at least 30 minutes.

4. Preheat the oven to 350°F [180°C].

5. Place the tart pan on a baking sheet and cover the dough with aluminum foil, shiny-side down. Bake for 20 minutes. Remove the foil and continue baking until lightly browned, 10 to 12 minutes. Remove from the oven and let cool completely.

cont.

TO MAKE THE CARAMEL FILLING:

1. In a medium saucepan, heat the heavy cream until warmed through. Remove from the burner and keep warm.

2. In another saucepan, combine the sugar, corn syrup, and ¼ cup [60 ml] water and heat over medium-high heat, swirling the pan to evenly cook the sugar. Do not stir with a spoon! This will cause the sugar to crystallize. Cook until the sugar syrup turns a deep amber color and just starts to smoke and the temperature reads 250°F [120°C] on a candy thermometer, 5 to 7 minutes. Remove from the heat and quickly whisk in the heated cream mixture. Add the butter and stir to combine. The mixture may bubble up and seize, so be careful. Stir, return to the heat, and cook over medium heat for another minute. Pour the caramel evenly into the crust and set aside for at least 45 minutes to set.

TO TOP AND SERVE:

1. Pour the ganache over the caramel layer and refrigerate for at least 30 minutes to allow it to set.

2. Let the tart sit at room temperature for at least 20 minutes before slicing and serving.

3. Keep leftovers stored in an airtight container in the fridge for up to 5 days (I like it best cold).

FOOD FOR THOUGHT:
Visualize the joy of taking that first bite. What will it taste like?

From Syria, with Love Cake

CAKE

1½ cups [210 g] all-purpose flour

½ cup [60 g] almond flour

1 tsp baking powder

1 tsp ground cardamom

½ tsp fine sea salt

1 cup [200 g] granulated sugar

½ cup [110 g] unsalted butter, at room temperature

3 Tbsp canola oil

2 eggs, at room temperature

Grated zest and juice of 1 lemon

1 tsp vanilla extract

½ tsp rose water

GLAZE

1½ cups [180 g] powdered sugar

2 Tbsp whole milk

TOPPING

¼ cup [30 g] chopped unsalted pistachios

¼ cup [35 g] pomegranate arils

2 to 3 Tbsp edible rose petals

3 lemon zest strips

SERVES 8

Syrians love to celebrate: weddings, births, holidays, a Tuesday. Honestly, we can find a reason to celebrate anything! This cake is a celebration all in itself. The vibrant colors and delicate flavors are so uplifting that you'll be transported on your fist bite. Celebration is inherently an act of love, so take a bite of this cake and celebrate yourself for making it. Go you!

TO MAKE THE CAKE:

1. Preheat the oven to 350°F [180°C]. Coat an 8 in [20 cm] round cake pan with nonstick cooking spray, line the pan with parchment paper, and spray again. Set the pan aside.

2. In a medium bowl, whisk the all-purpose flour, almond flour, baking powder, cardamom, and salt; set aside.

3. In the bowl of a stand mixer fitted with the paddle attachment, or in a medium bowl using a handheld electric mixer, beat the granulated sugar, butter, oil, and eggs until combined, 2 to 3 minutes. Add the lemon zest and juice, vanilla, and rose water. Turn the mixer to low, add the dry ingredients, and beat until just mixed.

4. Pour the batter into the prepared pan. Bake for 38 to 40 minutes, or until the cake is light brown on top and pulls away from the edges of the pan slightly. Let cool for 10 minutes and then turn out the cake onto a cooling rack.

cont.

TO MAKE THE GLAZE:

1. In a small bowl, whisk the powdered sugar and milk until thick ribbons form when you lift the whisk. Add extra milk by droplets if the glaze is too thick. Pour the glaze over the cooled cake.

TO TOP AND SERVE:

1. Decorate the cake with the pistachios, pomegranate arils, rose petals, and lemon zest strips in whatever pattern appeals to you.

2. Serve at room temperature, and store well-wrapped leftovers for up to 3 days at room temperature.

FOOD FOR THOUGHT:
Happiness is contagious. Seeing others happy uplifts me. How sweet is that?

Golden Tres Leches Cake

CAKE

1 cup [140 g] all-purpose flour

1½ tsp baking powder

¼ tsp fine sea salt

5 eggs, separated

1 cup [200 g] granulated sugar

⅓ cup [80 ml] whole milk

1 tsp vanilla extract

SOAKING LIQUID AND WHIPPED TOPPING

One 12 oz [340 g] can evaporated milk

One 14 oz [400 g] can sweetened condensed milk

1¾ cups [420 ml] heavy cream

1 tsp ground turmeric, plus more for sprinkling

½ tsp powdered ginger

½ tsp ground cinnamon

¼ tsp freshly ground black pepper

3 Tbsp powdered sugar

SERVES 12

Not only am I Syrian, but I'm also part Guatemalan (it's a fun fact that still surprises my friends). Grandma Raquel and Aunt Reina were born were in Guatemala, and this is their special recipe. They added healthy turmeric to the classic tres leches cake, essentially creating a golden milk cake. Turmeric is a natural antidepressant, so if the sugary milk doesn't make you happy, maybe the spice will provide a serotonin boost. This cake is perfect for literally any occasion: Make it on a Saturday for family and friends, or serve it for afternoon tea as a way to connect with loved ones.

TO MAKE THE CAKE:

1. Preheat the oven to 350°F [180°C]. Coat a 9 by 13 in [23 by 33 cm] baking pan with nonstick cooking spray (I prefer using glass Pyrex so you can see the yellow turmeric milk).

2. In a large bowl, whisk the flour, baking powder, and salt.

3. In the bowl of a stand mixer fitted with the paddle attachment, or in a medium bowl using a handheld electric mixer, beat the egg yolks and ¾ cup [150 g] of the granulated sugar on medium speed until the yolks become pale yellow. Add the milk and vanilla. On low speed, add the flour mixture and beat until just combined. Transfer the batter to a separate large bowl and clean the mixer.

cont.

4. In the bowl of the now-clean stand mixer, using the whisk attachment, beat the egg whites on medium speed until soft peaks form. Gradually add the remaining ¼ cup [50 g] of granulated sugar and beat until the egg whites are glossy and thick.

5. Gently fold the egg white mixture into the batter. It is OK if it is streaky. Pour the batter into the prepared pan and use an offset spatula to even out the top.

6. Bake for 40 minutes, or until it is golden brown and the sides pull away from the edges of the pan.

TO MAKE THE SOAKING LIQUID AND WHIPPED TOPPING:

1. In a saucepan, combine the evaporated milk, sweetened condensed milk, ¼ cup [60 ml] of the heavy cream, the turmeric, ginger, cinnamon, and pepper over medium-low heat. Heat for 4 to 5 minutes, or until the mixture is fragrant. Remove the pan from the heat and let cool.

2. Poke holes in the cake with a skewer every ½ in [13 mm] or so. Set aside 1 cup [240 ml] of the soaking liquid in the fridge (this will be used for the whipped topping), then slowly pour the rest of it over the cake (use a pastry brush to ensure that the liquid has soaked into all the skewer holes). Allow the cake to absorb the milk mixture for 20 minutes, then store in the fridge for at least 2 hours.

NOTE: *You can add chopped maraschino cherries as decoration if you want to be traditional.*

3. In the bowl of a stand mixer fitted with the whisk attachment, or in a medium bowl using a handheld electric mixer, beat the remaining 1½ cups [360 ml] of heavy cream and reserved 1 cup [240 ml] of soaking liquid. Add the powdered sugar and beat on medium speed until thick. Spread over the top of the cake. For extra golden color, sprinkle a bit of turmeric on top. Serve immediately.

TO SERVE:

1. This cake is best served the day it is made. Store leftovers in the fridge for up to 2 days.

FOOD FOR THOUGHT:
Experimentation can lead to new enjoyment. You'll never know what makes you happy unless you're willing to try new things.

Chocolate Ricotta Cake

CAKE

1¾ cups [245 g] all-purpose flour

1¼ cups [250 g] granulated sugar

1 cup [80 g] cocoa powder

2 tsp baking soda

1 tsp baking powder

½ tsp table salt

1¼ cups [300 g] ricotta cheese

½ cup [120 ml] coconut oil, melted

1 cup [240 ml] warm water,
about 110°F [45°C]

2 eggs plus 1 egg yolk

1 Tbsp vanilla extract

FROSTING

1 cup [220 g] unsalted butter,
at room temperature

⅜ cup [90 g] ricotta cheese

½ cup [40 g] cocoa powder

1 tsp vanilla extract

1 tsp espresso powder

½ tsp table salt

2½ cups [300 g] powdered sugar

SERVES 8

Sometimes you hear a flavor pairing and go, "What were they thinking?!" But hear me out. Chocolate and ricotta are amazing together. I'm not joking. They're the ingredient couple you didn't know you needed in your life until now. This cake is perfect for both chocolate and cheese lovers. The ricotta adds a beautiful creamy texture to the cake and the frosting, while the chocolate is, well, chocolate! It's decadent and rich in all the right ways. One bite and you'll be smiling.

TO MAKE THE CAKE:

1. Preheat the oven to 350°F [180°C]. Spray two 9 in [23 cm] round cake pans with nonstick cooking spray.

2. In a large bowl, whisk the flour, granulated sugar, cocoa powder, baking soda, baking powder, and salt. Set aside.

3. In a medium bowl, whisk the ricotta cheese, coconut oil, warm water, eggs, egg yolk, and vanilla. Make sure that the water is warm so that it will keep the coconut oil melted and help break up the ricotta cheese. Whisk the wet ingredients into the dry until a consistent, smooth batter forms.

4. Divide the batter evenly between the two cake pans and bake for 30 minutes, or until the center of the cakes are set.

TOPPING

Mini semisweet or dark
chocolate chips

5. Set the cakes aside to cool for 30 minutes, then remove them from their pans and allow them to cool completely on cooling racks.

TO MAKE THE FROSTING AND ASSEMBLE:

1. While the cakes cool, in clean mixing bowl, use a handheld electric mixer to cream the butter and ricotta cheese until fluffy. Next, beat in the cocoa powder, vanilla, espresso powder, and salt. Finally, add the powdered sugar, ½ cup [60 g] at a time, beating the mixture on medium speed and scraping the sides of the bowl down each time.

2. Decorate the cake with the chocolate chips and serve. Store covered in the fridge for up to 4 days.

FOOD FOR THOUGHT:
Find joy in the process of baking. Even if the final product isn't what you expected, there are still things you may have learned or enjoyed throughout.

Rainbow Pride Cupcakes

CUPCAKES

1¾ cups [245 g] all-purpose flour

1 cup [120 g] cake flour

1 Tbsp baking powder

½ tsp fine sea salt

1½ cups [300 g] granulated sugar

½ cup [110 g] unsalted butter,
at room temperature

½ cup [120 ml] canola oil

4 eggs, at room temperature

1 Tbsp vanilla extract

1¼ cups [300 ml] buttermilk

FROSTING

1¾ cup [385 g] unsalted butter,
at room temperature

7 cups [840 g] powdered sugar

2½ tsp vanilla extract

Pinch of salt

3 or 4 Tbsp [44 or 59 ml]
whole milk or heavy cream

Food coloring (optional)

cont.

MAKES 24 CUPCAKES

Put down the flour. Set aside the mixing bowl. Take a moment to really internalize what I am about to say: Always celebrate who you are. Got it? Are you sure? Good.

As humans, we experience shame in numerous ways, be it our religion, race, sexuality, or even how we handled our last decision (Lord knows I have). And with so many communities, or parts of our selves to juggle, it can feel like a never-ending struggle. These cupcakes are the antidote to shame; they're a celebration of self, whatever that self may be. Did you know that rainbows literally contain the entire spectrum of visible light? That's why it's been adopted as a symbol of the LGBTQ+ community, as a way to celebrate the diversity of our community.

So let's make these cupcakes and defy that shame. Integrate the colors the same way you integrate all your identities. Melding all of your "selves" together might be tough, but rainbows are a testament to resilience—they always appear after the storm!

TO MAKE THE CUPCAKES:

1. Preheat the oven to 350°F [180°C]. Coat the top of a muffin tin with nonstick cooking spray and then line the cups with paper liners. Set aside.

2. In a large bowl, whisk the all-purpose flour, cake flour, baking powder, and salt.

cont.

DECORATIONS

Sprinkles (optional)

Rainbow candies

FOOD FOR THOUGHT:
You're allowed to enjoy your
existence. Let go of your shame
and embrace yourself. Don't
let anyone, or anything, dim
your light.

3. In the bowl of a stand mixer fitted with the paddle attachment, or in a medium bowl using a handheld electric mixer, beat the granulated sugar, butter, and canola oil until well combined. Add the eggs, one at a time, mixing after each addition and scraping down the bowl with a rubber spatula as needed. Add the vanilla and mix to just combine.

4. Add one-third of the flour mixture and then add half the buttermilk, alternating between the two and ending with the flour mixture. Stir until just combined, but don't overmix!

5. Divide the batter evenly among the paper liners and bake for 20 to 23 minutes, or until the cupcakes are lightly golden and bounce back when touched. Let cool for 10 minutes, then turn out onto a cooling rack to cool completely.

TO MAKE THE FROSTING AND SERVE:

1. In the bowl of a stand mixer fitted with the whisk attachment, or in a large bowl using a handheld electric mixer with whisks, beat the butter for 7 to 8 minutes on medium-high speed, or until fluffy and pale, then lower to medium speed and add the powdered sugar 1 cup [120 g] at a time. Let it incorporate between each addition. Add the vanilla, salt, milk, and food coloring. Whip on high speed for 3 to 4 minutes, or until creamy and fluffy. Immediately spread frosting on each cupcake and decorate as desired with sprinkles and rainbow candies. Store leftovers in the fridge for up to 2 days.

ACKNOWLEDGMENTS

To Michael Harari, I am forever grateful to call you a friend and coauthor of this book. You showed up for me through it all (and I do mean all): countless hours spent on JackBakes, writing and editing this book, and supporting all the crazy ideas that popped into my head. You have been my voice of reason, and I don't know what I would've done without your support.

Thank you to Chronicle Books, especially my editor extraordinaire Cristina Garces. You took a chance on a first-time author with a big idea and helped bring Baking Therapy to life in this book. A special thank you to Dena Rayess for infusing my personality into this project (I know it was no easy task). Additional thanks to Rachel Harrell and Karen Levy.

Thanks to my literary agent, Sarah Smith. You recognized the potential in this idea and helped me put my best desserts forward. Your guidance along the way was greatly appreciated.

To my fabulous recipe contributors who sprinkled their magic into this book—Cori Rupe, Lior Idelson, Rachael Pilaski, and Mikaela Bloom— you all have a special place in my heart and kitchen. The recipes you developed are *chef's kiss*; I know people will love baking them.

To Pam Eisenberg-Kohl, thank you for your unconditional love and guidance. You've been my guardian angel.

To Murray Hidary, Sarah Ivanhoe, and Hoda Mahmoodzadegan: You each gave me hope for the future, prepared me for success, and have been constant rocks in my life.

To Simone Antar Ruiz, who taught me patience and dedication. You have been an integral part of my educational journey, and I will be forever grateful for all you have done.

To Vinceta Reeves, I was blessed to have you be like a second mother. I'll never forget your "stick-to-it-ivity" to keep going, even when things get tough.

To psychiatrist Dr. Matthew Goulet, you were always someone I could count on during my transformative years and well into adulthood. Your insight helped me prepare for success.

Every therapist should have a therapist. To my rock, Debbie Antar: You went above and beyond the traditional role. You helped me through the chaos to find my potential.

To Pete Ross, you've helped the oven light bulb go off. It's been quite an adventure together.

To all of my friends, it means so much to me that you're cheering me on and pushing me to be the best version of myself in everything I do.

Great Grandma Sarah Benun (a.k.a. Grandma Benun), thank you for teaching me about the importance of "community through carbs" and the art of hospitality.

To my wonderful aunts: Aunt Brenda, thank you for teaching me how to bake with all the TLC I can give. "I'm your biggest fan." Aunt Cheryl, you set an example for how to live authentically. Thank you for always reminding me of who I really am. Aunt Dina, you were my inspiration for becoming a therapist, and you've been an advocate and support system through all junctures in my life.

To my siblings Albert, Margaux, and Raquel, thank you for putting up with my antics over the years. I love you all.

Grandma Raquel, we're each other's happy pills. You, along with Grandpa Jack, instilled in me the importance of culture and embracing our family history. Te amo.

Grandma Peggy and Grandpa Albert, you always thought I was going to be someone special. Seeing you smile whenever I entered a room was a constant reminder of your love and my potential to do anything. I know wherever you are, you're smiling. I miss you every day.

To my father, you have my utmost respect. You taught me the recipe for life: that honesty, integrity, and generosity can help you reach the stars—a place you always thought I belonged. Thank you for creating a path for me.

Mom, you taught me by example through your innovative and forward-thinking cooking. You believed in me and always stood by my side through thick and thin. So, I can safely say I know I'm your favorite and you're mine.

— A —

almonds
Manifesting Cookie Bars, 244–45
No-Bake Cashew "Cheesecake,"
146–47
Pick-Me-Up Granola, 163
aniseed, in Ka'ak (Round Mediterranean Crackers), 115–17
Apples, Baked, with Crumble Topping, 52–54
Aunt Barbara's Mandel Bread, 68–69

— B —

Bagels, New York-Style, 180–81
Bakery-Style Cinnamon Swirl Bread with Raisins, 182–83
Baking Meditation, 61
Baking Therapy, 8–9, 16–17, 26, 134, 135, 204
banana(s)
Stress-less Banana Pudding Trifle, 152–54
Upside-Down Pineapple Pound Cake, 108–9
You've Met Your (Banana) Matcha Loaf, 164
bars
Chai-Soaked Pear Shortbread Bars, 88–89
Manifesting Cookie Bars, 244–45
Tahini Blondies, 45
berries
Fruit Muffins, 123–24
Lemon Blueberry Scones, 93–94
Limoncello Tiramisu in a Glass, 222–24
No-Bake Cashew "Cheesecake,"
146–47
Not-Your-Ordinary Blackberry Cobbler, 141–42
Slice-and-Bake Raspberry Pecan Cookies, 43–44
Summer Fruit Crumbles, 66
Better Than Sex Cake, 30–33
Biscuits, Soft and Flaky, 190–91
bittersweet chocolate, in Mini Thumbprint Cookies, 195–96
Blondies, Tahini, 45
Blueberry Lemon Scones, 93–94
Boost-of-Energy Coconut Lime Bites, 36
Bread Pudding, Challah Caramel, 123–24
bread(s) and rolls
Bakery-Style Cinnamon Swirl Bread with Raisins, 182–83
Chocolate Chip Babka Crunch, 137–40
Jack's Famous Challah, 104–7
New York-Style Bagels, 180–81

Pecan Cinnamon Rolls, 177–79
Pesto Pull-Apart Bread, 218–19
Slap-It-Together Focaccia, 198–99
You've Met Your (Banana) Matcha Loaf, 164
Breadsticks, Marbled Rye, 73–76
brownies
Cookies and Cream Brownies, 225–26
Trifecta of Comfort Ice Cream Sandwiches, 128–29
Bundt Cake, Lemon Ginger, 83–84

— C —

cakes
Better Than Sex Cake, 30–33
Chocolate Ricotta Cake, 262–63
Confetti Pound Cake, 241–43
Five-Star Meringue Birthday Cake, 148–51
From Syria, with Love Cake, 255–57
Golden Tres Leches Cake, 258–61
Grapefruit White Chocolate Yogurt Cake, 249–50
Heaven and Hell Cake, 90–92
I Crumble for You Coffee Cake, 211–12
Jumpin' Java Cake, 213–14
Lemon Ginger Bundt Cake, 83–84
Lime Chiffon Cake, 77–80
Self Care in a Cup Cake, 35
Syrian Carrot Cake, 232–33
Upside-Down Pineapple Pound Cake, 108–9
Caramel Buttercream, in Better Than Sex Cake, 30–33
Caramel Filling, in Twix Tart, 253–54
Caramel Sauce
Better Than Sex Cake, 30–33
Challah Caramel Bread Pudding, 123–24
caraway seeds, in Marbled Rye Breadsticks, 73–76
Carrot Cake, Syrian, 232–33
cashews
Boost-of-Energy Coconut Lime Bites, 36
No-Bake Cashew "Cheesecake,"
146–47
Chai tea, in Chai-Soaked Pear Shortbread Bars, 88–89
Challah Caramel Bread Pudding, 123–24
Challah, Jack's Famous, 104–7
cheese. See also Parmesan cheese; ricotta cheese
asiago, in Pesto Pull-Apart Bread, 218–19

gruyère, in Mushroom and Gruyère Quiche, 46–48
Sambusak (Braided Cheese Pastries), 118–20
Savory Cheddar and Chive Scone, 93–94
cheesecakes
Cheesecake with a Pomegranate Twist, 192–94
No-Bake Cashew "Cheesecake,"
146–47
chia seeds
Boost-of-Energy Coconut Lime Bites, 36
Fruit Muffins, 123–24
No-Bake Cashew "Cheesecake,"
146–47
Chocolate Chip Muffins, 123–24
chocolate chips or chunks. See also semisweet chocolate and semisweet chocolate chips
Chocolate Chip Babka Crunch, 137–40
It's My Cookie and I'll Share If I Want To, 49–51
Chocolate Ganache
Better Than Sex Cake, 30–33
Jack's Chocolate Chip Cookies, 184–86
Peanut Butter Pretzel Pie, 38–40
recipe, 30–31
Twix Tart, 253–54
Chocolate Ricotta Cake, 262–63
chocolate-hazelnut spread
Chocolate-Hazelnut Mousse Pie, 155–58
Churros with, 173–76
Churros, 173–76
Cinnamon-Sugar Churros, 173–76
Soft Pretzel Triangles, 187–89
Cobbler, Not-Your-Ordinary Blackberry, 141–42
coconut
Boost-of-Energy Coconut Lime Bites, 36
Five-Star Meringue Birthday Cake, 148–51
Grapefruit White Chocolate Yogurt Cake, 249–50
Manifesting Cookie Bars, 244–45
Tropical Fruit Tart, 208–9
Coconut Lime Bites, Boost-of-Energy, 36
coconut milk, in Five-Star Meringue Birthday Cake, 148–51
coffee/coffee granules
Chocolate-Hazelnut Mousse Pie, 155–58
Jumpin' Java Cake, 213–14
Confetti Pound Cake, 241–43

connection with others, 202–5
Cookie Dough, Eat-All-You-Want
    Edible, 55
cookies
    Aunt Brenda's Rose Water Chews,
        65
    in Cookies and Cream Brownies,
        225–26
    in Stress-less Banana Pudding
        Trifle, 152–54
    It's My Cookie and I'll Share If I
        Want To, 49–51
    Lemon and Lavender Cookies,
        247–48
    Let's Go on a Date (-Stuffed) Cook-
        ies, 229–31
    Mini Thumbprint Cookies, 195–96
    Red Velvet Cookies with Cream
        Cheese Glaze, 121–22
    Slice-and-Bake Raspberry Pecan
        Cookies, 43–44
    Take Me to Chocolate Heaven
        Cookies, 221
    Want S'mores Cookies?, 215–17
Cornbread Muffins, 227–28
Crackers, Round Mediterranean
    (Ka'ak), 115–17
cream cheese
    Cheesecake with a Pomegranate
        Twist, 192–94
    Peanut Butter Pretzel Pie, 38–40
    Pecan Cinnamon Rolls, 177–79
    Red Velvet Cookies with Cream
        Cheese Glaze, 121–22
    Syrian Carrot Cake, 232–33
crumb toppings
    Chocolate Chip Babka Crunch,
        137–40
    Cinnamon Chocolate Chip Crumb
        Muffins, 251–52
    I Crumble for You Coffee Cake,
        211–12
    Individual Baked Apples, 52–54
    Summer Fruit Crumble, 66
Cupcakes, Rainbow Pride, 265–66

— D —
dark chocolate/chocolate chips
    Chocolate Ricotta Cake, 262–63
    Grandma Raquel's Dark Chocolate
        Mousse, 81–82
    Jack's Chocolate Chip Cookies,
        184–86
    Vanilla Bean Panna Cotta, 160–62
dates
    Boost-of-Energy Coconut Lime
        Bites, 36

Let's Go on a Date (-Stuffed) Cook-
    ies, 229–31
No-Bake Cashew "Cheesecake,"
    146–47
Syrian Carrot Cake, 232–33
Donuts, Baked Pumpkin, 85–86
dulce de leche, Churos with, 173–76

— E —
eggs, in Mushroom and Gruyère
    Quiche, 46–48
Espinoza, Rudy, 133
espresso powder
    Chocolate Ricotta Cake, 262–63
    Cookies and Cream Brownies,
        225–26
Exelbert, Renee, 15, 61

— F —
flaxseed
    Boost-of-Energy Coconut Lime
        Bites, 36
    Fruit Muffins, 123–24
    Manifesting Cookie Bars, 244–45
    Want S'mores Cookies? (vegan),
        217
Focaccia, Slap-It-Together, 198–99
Fritters, Lemon Ricotta, 206
Fruit Crumbles, Summer, 66
Fruit Muffins, 123–24
frustration, 168–72

— G —
Galette, Feelin' Peachy, 143–45
gelatin, in Vanilla Bean Panna Cotta,
    160–62
ginger, in Lemon Ginger Bundt Cake,
    83–84
gluten-free crust, 46
graham crackers
    Manifesting Cookie Bars, 244–45
    Want S'mores Cookies?, 215–17
Grandma Peggy's Kanafeh, 112–14
Grandma Raquel's Dark Chocolate
    Mousse, 81–82
Granola, Pick-Me-Up, 163
Grapefruit White Chocolate Yogurt
    Cake, 249–50

— H —
Homemade Whipped Cream
    Confetti Pound Cake, 241–43
    Feelin' Peachy Galette with, 143–45
    Individual Baked Apples with
        Crumble Topping, 52–54
    Lime Chiffon Cake, 77–80
    Peanut Butter Pretzel Pie, 38–40

recipe, 39–40
Sicilian Orange Semolina Cake, 159
honey
    Honey-Roasted Pistachios, 80
    Lime Chiffon Cake, 77–80
    The Not-So-Rough Puff Pear
        Pastry, 71–72
    Warm Cornbread Muffins, 227–28
    You've Met Your (Banana) Matcha
        Loaf, 164

— I —
ice cream
    Individual Baked Apples with
        Crumble Topping, 54
    Trifecta of Comfort Ice Cream
        Sandwiches, 128–29

— J —
Jack's Chocolate Chip Cookies, 184–86
Jack's Famous Challah, 104–7
JackBakes, 15, 133
Joy Baking, 237–38
Junior Mint candies, in Mini Thumb-
    print Cookies, 195–96

— K —
Ka'ak (Round Mediterranean Crack-
    ers), 115–17
Kabat-Zinn, Jon, 62
Kahlúa, in Grandma Raquel's Dark
    Chocolate Mousse, 81–82
Kanafeh, Grandma Peggy's, 112–14
kiwis, in Tropical Fruit Tart, 208–9

— L —
ladyfingers, in Limoncello Tiramisu in
    a Glass, 222–24
lavender (culinary), in Lemon and
    Lavender Cookies, 247–48
lemon curd, in Limoncello Tiramisu
    in a Glass, 222–24
lemon juice/zest
    Cheesecake with a Pomegranate
        Twist, 192–94
    From Syria, with Love Cake,
        255–57
    Lemon and Lavender Cookies,
        247–48
    Lemon Blueberry Scone, 93–94
    Lemon Ginger Bundt Cake, 83–84
    Lemon Ricotta Fritters, 206
    Limoncello Tiramisu in a Glass,
        222–24
lime
    Boost-of-Energy Coconut Lime
        Bites, 36

Lime Chiffon Cake, 77–80
Summer Fruit Crumbles, 66
Limoncello Tiramisu in a Glass,
222–24

— M —
Madonna, 14
Mandel Bread, Aunt Barbara's, 68–69
mangoes
Summer Fruit Crumbles, 66
Tropical Fruit Tart, 208–9
maple syrup
Baked Pumpkin Donuts to Fall For,
85–86
Maple Walnut Scones, 93–94
Pick-Me-Up Granola, 163
Marbled Rye Breadsticks, 73–76
marshmallow creme
Heaven and Hell Cake, 90–92
Peanut Butter Pretzel Pie, 38–40
marshmallows, in Want S'mores
Cookies?, 215–17
mascarpone
Limoncello Tiramisu in a Glass,
222–24
Tropical Fruit Tart, 208–9
matcha powder, in You've Met Your
(Banana) Matcha Loaf, 164
Meditation, Baking, 61
meringue
Aunt Brenda's Pistachio Water
Chews, 65
Five-Star Meringue Birthday Cake,
148–51
Middle Eastern Rice Pudding, 126–27
mindfulness, 58–63
Mini Thumbprint Cookies, 195–96
mise en place, 8–9, 19–20, 172
mousse
Chocolate-Hazelnut Mousse Pie,
155–58
Grandma Raquel's Dark Chocolate
Mousse, 81–82
muffins
Choose Your Own Stud Muffins,
110–11
Cinnamon Chocolate Chip Crumb
Muffins, 251–52
Warm Cornbread Muffins, 227–28
mug, cake in a, 35
Mushroom and Gruyère Quiche, 46–48

— N —
nectarines, in Summer Fruit Crumbles, 66
nuts. *See* almonds; cashews; pecans;
pistachios; walnuts

— O —
orange blossom water
Grandma Peggy's Kanafeh, 112–14
Homemade Whipped Cream, 39
Let's Go on a Date (-Stuffed) Cook-
ies, 229–31
Lime Chiffon Cake, 77–80
Sicilian Orange Semolina Cake, 159
Vanilla Bean Panna Cotta, 160–62
orange zest/juice
Aunt Barbara's Mandel Bread,
68–69
Pick-Me-Up Granola, 163
Sicilian Orange Semolina Cake, 159
Vanilla Bean Panna Cotta, 160–62
Oreos, in Cookies and Cream Brown-
ies, 225–26

— P —
Panna Cotta, Vanilla Bean, 160–62
pantry staples, 20
Parmesan cheese
Mushroom and Gruyère Quiche,
46–48
Pesto Pull-Apart Bread, 218–19
peaches, in Feelin' Peachy Galette,
143–45
Peanut Butter Pretzel Pie, 38–40
pears
Chai-Soaked Pear Shortbread
Bars, 88–89
The Not-So-Rough Puff Pear
Pastry, 71–72
pecans
Better Than Sex Cake, 30–33
I Crumble for You Coffee Cake,
211–12
Pecan Cinnamon Rolls, 177–79
Slice-and-Bake Raspberry Pecan
Cookies, 43–44
Syrian Carrot Cake, 232–33
Pesto Pull-Apart Bread, 218–19
phylo dough (shredded), in Grandma
Peggy's Kanafeh, 112–14
pies
Chocolate-Hazelnut Mousse Pie,
155–58
Peanut Butter Pretzel Pie, 38–40
pineapple
Five-Star Meringue Birthday Cake,
148–51
Upside-Down Pineapple Pound
Cake, 108–9
pistachios
Aunt Brenda's Pistachio Rose
Water Chews, 65
From Syria, with Love Cake,
255–57

Lime Chiffon Cake, 77–80
Middle Eastern Rice Pudding,
126–27
pomegranate arils, in From Syria,
with Love Cake, 255–57
pomegranate sauce, in Cheesecake
with a Pomegranate Twist, 192–94
pound cakes
Confetti Pound Cake, 241–43
Upside-Down Pineapple Pound
Cake, 108–9
Pretzel Pie, Peanut Butter, 38–40
Pretzel Triangles, 187–89
pudding
Better Than Sex Cake, 30–33
Middle Eastern Rice Pudding,
126–27
Stress-less Banana Pudding Trifle,
152–54
puff pastry, in The Not-So-Rough Puff
Pear Pastry, 71–72
Pumpkin Donuts to Fall For, 85–86
pumpkin seeds
Baked Pumpkin Donuts to Fall For,
85–86
Pick-Me-Up Granola, 163

— Q —
Quiche, Mushroom and Gruyère,
46–48

— R —
Rainbow Pride Cupcakes, 265–66
rainbow sprinkles/candies
Confetti Muffins, 123–24
Confetti Pound Cake, 241–43
Rainbow Pride Cupcakes, 265–66
Raisins, Bakery-Style Cinnamon Swirl
Bread with, 182–83
Raspberry Pecan Cookies, Slice-and-
Bake, 43–44
Red Velvet Cookies with Cream
Cheese Glaze, 121–22
Rice Pudding, Middle Eastern, 126–27
ricotta cheese
Chocolate Ricotta Cake, 262–63
Grandma Peggy's Kanafeh, 112–14
Lemon and Lavender Cookies,
247–48
Lemon Ricotta Fritters, 206
rolled oats
Pick-Me-Up Granola, 163
Summer Fruit Crumble, 66
Rolls, Pecan Cinnamon, 177–79
rose petals (edible), in From Syria,
with Love Cake, 255–57

rose water
    Aunt Brenda's Rose Water Chews, 65
    From Syria, with Love Cake, 255–57
    Grandma Peggy's Kanafeh, 112–14
    Homemade Whipped Cream, 39
    in Syrian baking, 99
    Let's Go on a Date(-Stuffed) Cookies, 229–31
    Middle Eastern Rice Pudding, 126–27
    Syrian baking and, 99
rosemary
    Mushroom and Gruyère Quiche, 46–48
    Slap-It-Together Focaccia, 198–99
    The Not-So-Rough Puff Pear Pastry, 71–72

— S —
S'mores Cookies, 215–217
Sambusak (Braided Cheese Pastries), 118–20
Scones, Choose-Your-Own, 93–94
Self Care in a Cup Cake, 35
self-care, 23–27
semisweet chocolate and semisweet chocolate chips
    Aunt Barbara's Mandel Bread, 68–69
    Better Than Sex Cake, 30–33
    Challah Caramel Bread Pudding, 123–24
    Chocolate Chip Babka Crunch, 137–40
    Cinnamon Chocolate Chip Crumb Muffins, 251–52
    Cookies and Cream Brownies, 225–26
    Jack's Chocolate Chip Cookies, 184–86
    Manifesting Cookie Bars, 244–45
    Trifecta of Comfort Ice Cream Sandwiches, 128–29
    Want S'mores Cookies?, 215–17
Semolina Cake, Sicilian Orange, 159
sesame seeds
    Ka'ak (Round Mediterranean Crackers), 115–17
    Sambusak (Braided Cheese Pastries), 118–20
    Tahini Blondies, 45
shiva, sitting, 98, 99–100
Sicilian Orange Semolina Cake, 159
Slice-and-Bake Raspberry Pecan Cookies, 43–44

Soft Pretzel Triangles, 187–89
sour cream
    Better Than Sex Cake, 30–31
    Cinnamon Chocolate Chip Crumb Muffins, 251–52
    Confetti Pound Cake, 241–43
    I Crumble for You Coffee Cake, 211–12
    Lemon Ginger Bundt Cake, 83–84
    Syrian Carrot Cake, 232–33
    Upside-Down Pineapple Pound Cake, 108–9
    Warm Cornbread Muffins, 227–28
spinach, in Mushroom and Gruyère Quiche, 46–48
strawberries, in No-Bake Cashew "Cheesecake," 146–47
stress(es), 132–35
Stress-less Banana Pudding Trifle, 152–54
sunflower seeds, in Pick-Me-Up Granola, 163
Syrian Carrot Cake, 232–33
Syrian Jewish community, 9, 11–14

— T —
Tahini Blondies, 45
tarts
    Tropical Fruit Tart, 208–9
    Twix Tart, 253–54
therapy, baking and, 14, 15–16
Tres Leches Cake, Golden, 258–61
Trifle, Stress-less Banana Pudding, 152–54
Tropical Fruit Tart, 208–09
Twix Tart, 253–54

— U —
Upside-Down Pineapple Pound Cake, 108–9

— V —
vanilla bean paste
    Stress-less Banana Pudding Trifle, 152–54
    Vanilla Bean Panna Cotta, 160–62
vegan recipes
    Eat-All-You-Want Edible Cookie Dough, 55
    Jumpin' Java Cake, 213–14
    Not-Your-Ordinary Blackberry Cobbler, 141–42
    Want S'mores Cookies, 217

— W —
walnuts
    Aunt Barbara's Mandel Bread, 68–69
    Individual Baked Apples, 52–54
    Let's Go on a Date (-Stuffed) Cookies, 229–31
    Maple Walnut Scones, 93–94
whipped cream. See also Homemade Whipped Cream
    Cheesecake with a Pomegranate Twist, 192–94
    Limoncello Tiramisu in a Glass, 222–24
    Stress-less Banana Pudding Trifle, 152–54
    Tropical Fruit Tart, 208–9
white chocolate and white chocolate chips
    Cookies and Cream Brownies, 225–26
    Grapefruit White Chocolate Yogurt Cake, 249–50
    Jack's Chocolate Chip Cookies, 184–86
    Mini Thumbprint Cookies, 195–96
    Pick-Me-Up Granola, 163
    Red Velvet Cookies with Cream Cheese Glaze, 121–22

— Y —
yogurt
    Choose Your Own Stud Muffins, 110–11
    Grapefruit White Chocolate Yogurt Cake, 249–50
    Sicilian Orange Semolina Cake, 159
    Soft and Flaky Biscuits, 190–91

Cover design by Rachel Harrell.